JENNYLYN HART

❦

CELEBRATING LIFE
ONE STEP AT A TIME

❦

Jenny's
Journeys

MORGAN JAMES PUBLISHING • NEW YORK

Jenny's Journeys

Copyright ©2007 Jennylyn Hart

Paperback ISBN: 978-1-60037-256-8
Hardcover ISBN: 978-1-60037-302-2
Audio ISBN: 978-1-60037-305-3

Published by:

MORGAN · JAMES
THE ENTREPRENEURIAL PUBLISHER ™
www.morganjamespublishing.com

Morgan James Publishing, LLC
1225 Franklin Ave Ste 32
Garden City, NY 11530-1693
Toll Free 800-485-4943
www.MorganJamesPublishing.com

Cover/Interior Design by:

Rachel Campbell
rachel@r2cdesign.com

Dedicated to

To my Angel, Rachel

& my husband, Chris

Acknowledgements

THERE ARE SO MANY PEOPLE that have touched my life in so many ways that a mere mention here is minor in comparison to the great ways they have touched me.

First and foremost, Mom, you are the best mom and I love you for everything you have done for me and the rest of my family! I appreciate all the sacrifices you made over the years they did not go unnoticed.

Thanks to you, Dad, for showing me God is always there.

Thanks to my husband, Chris, for not leaving when all the chips were stacked against us. Especially thanks for creating our Angel together!

Thank you, Rachel, my angel. You are the reason I get out of my bed and thank God for another day of smiling with you!

Thanks to you, Judy, my cousin, for helping me get in and out of the tub when I couldn't do it myself! ☺

Acknowledgements ⁓ *Jenny's Journeys*

Thank you goes to the rest of my family for being there when I needed you most.

Thank you, Dr. Thomas Behr, who told me I had a story that needed to be written and encouraged me every step of the way.

Thank you, Ifida Known, Barb Veselich, Jane-Marie Sandberg, John Childers and his team, Carolyn, Ben & David and the rest of the team from Morgan James for believing in my story and all those who provided me with the support to produce this journey.

Thank you all for appearing on the "next page" when I had a new decision to make.

"Invalid leads to Invalid"

By J. Soler, age 16

Invalid…

Ignored…

Minute…

Minor…

Worse…

Anger…

Fear….!

Inability that never existed,

Has made me look at life again,

Put me in an awkward position,

Caused me to rely on others,

Realize the things taken for granted.

And for the time being produced an Invalid.

Table of Contents

Foreword

"**DO YOU BELIEVE IN MIRACLES?**" These five simple words united a nation as a group of 20 unknown amateur and collegiate hockey players did what a team of professional All Stars couldn't do, they rocked the world by beating "Goliath" in Lake Placid, New York on February 22, 1980.

As I sit in my office and look around me, I am motivated and inspired by the many photographs and inspirational sayings: "CHANGE" "Do not pray for an easy life. Pray to be a strong person." "No one knows what it is he can do till he tries –Syrus." "You don't have to have the lead if you have the courage to come from behind." My favorite is "ACTION – It only takes a single thought to move the world." Our thoughts coupled with our actions are expressed in what we have created for ourselves in the world in which we call LIFE.

Don't like the life you've been dealt? Then change it! Albert Einstein is attributed for saying, "Insanity: doing the same thing over and over again and expecting different results." Are you happy with your life today? Don't question God or blame anyone else. Only you have the power to make it a great day – so go out and do it! Just like my friend Jenny does. Hers is a journey of change, of persistence, of inspiration, of motivation, of success, of action.

It is through the success habits you implement in your life on a consistent basis that trigger your abundance. Taking the simple, baby-steps correctly each day will unlock your future and assist you in creating the personal achievement you desire for your life regardless of your abilities. Don't allow the nay-sayers or dream stealers to label you or tell you – you can't do something or you aren't good enough, or you just don't have what it takes… You've heard them all. Just don't believe them. Don't buy into their negativity. Don't allow their perceived realities to become your own.

Just imagine where we would be today if Herb Brooks, Mother Teresa, Don Haskins, Barbara McClintock, Sam Walton, Dr. Charles R. Drew, Ray Kroc, Martin Luther King, Jr., Bill Gates, Montel Williams, Mahatma Gandhi or any others who have changed the world through persistence, positive attitude, passion, drive, motivation, and most importantly - action - had listened to the dream stealers in their lives?

The simple definition of the word "HERO" is defined: 1) Someone who acts to help another with no thought for herself or himself. 2) Someone who is admired for achievements or noble qualities. Nowhere does it say we must be famous, wealthy, a specific age, of royal descent, or be in prime health. A hero is one who acts, one who is admired for their achievements; one who helps others! Jenny Hart is an everyday hero. This mom, wife, daughter, sister, author, former EMT, lifeguard and community association president shares with you the motivating insights of her life and journeys learning about, living with, and overcoming the obstacles of what some consider "a life sentence."

Do you believe in miracles? This powerful journey of one woman's experiences in conquering her "Goliath" and making the most out of her life, as she knows each and every one of us can too, regardless of the hand life has dealt us, is a wonderful example of the power and potential of the human spirit put into action.

Enjoy the journey,

IFIDA KNOWN

Author, Speaker, Consultant, Infopreneur

Success Habits That Trigger Abundance

www.IfidaKnown.com

Introduction

DREAM STEALERS AND NAYSAYERS IN my life said I would never walk again; never talk again. "You can't do that. Nobody's done that before." Where would I be today, if I had listened ...

One minute you think everything is beautiful – that nothing could ever go wrong. Then, the next minute, as if someone is watching you, thinking your life is too perfect, the story changes.

I'm not sure where or when this story starts or even how it might end, but it is a story I will tell nonetheless. You, my friend, have caught my story in the middle somewhere or possibly toward its end. No one can really say for sure because *life is funny that way.*

When I was a little girl, my parents said I could be anything I wanted to be. They said I could do whatever I wanted to do with my life. They were happy I was healthy and normal. When I was born, I had all ten fingers and all ten toes. I didn't have anything wrong. In their eyes, I was perfect.

When I was a little kid, I enjoyed puzzles. My mom tells me I was given puzzles with the frame. You know the kind that the shape of the piece that belongs in that spot was actually outlined on the cardboard backing. My mom tells me I never found putting the puzzles back together in the frame challenging enough. As a matter of fact, she tells me I would take all these puzzles apart, mix them together and put them back together upside down with the blank cardboard side facing up.

I went to school like everyone else. I learned to read. I enjoyed reading. I enjoyed doing puzzles. So it was no surprise when I discovered those "choose your own adventure" books where you decided how the story continued and then how it ended; I read everyone I could get my hands on.

You may not have read these books but let me tell you a little about these books. Here is a quick example, a little girl is given a present. It is a lovely square box wrapped in shiny gold paper with a beautiful silver ribbon. (If you want it to be a piece of jewelry, go to the next page. If you want it to be a rag doll, go to page twenty.)

I loved those "Choose your own Adventure" books. I would read them over and over making a different choice each time I read it so I could make the story end in a different way. Who knew I would actually be living one; well, not really.

In my living-adventure I don't get to choose which way I want or wanted some of the journeys in the adventure to turn. I just have to keep going to find out how each page turns because something else is writing each new page for me.

Different characters appear in my living-adventure to help me figure out what decision to make, which page I should turn to next. Some make the right choice or at least they look like the right choice at the time. Some times they said I should have gotten the jewelry and other times they said I got the rag doll. Either way this living-adventure book talks about all these journeys and how they've concluded for me. Sometimes through choices I made. Sometimes through choices others, people or circumstances, made for me.

I would like to take this opportunity to invite YOU to make a choice. I would like to invite you to read about my journeys in whatever order you choose.

Here are your choices…

If you want to read about how this adventure started go to

If you want to read about the journeys in this adventure go to

If you want to read about how I chose to accept this adventure go to

If you want to just read about how the adventure will end go to

I'm not sure where your curiosity lies. Maybe you are a person who likes to know how it ends before you hear about where it all started. Or maybe you just want to read about all the little excursions along the entire journey. Or maybe you want to read about all the letters that surround my life. Or maybe you want to read the whole story from being to end. Anyway you choose it is your decision.

I hope you accept my invitation to read about all of the journeys in this living-adventure story. I promise when you get to the end of this book there will be another decision for you to make. Maybe you have had similar journeys in your life or maybe you know someone else who has letters following them around.

Anyway you look at it, just know you never travel alone.

PHASE I

THE MYSTERY
OF THE FALL

THE BIG GAME

Welcome Back! We are back at the NJ Girls' High School Varsity Basketball State Championship game during the final minutes of the fourth quarter. This game has been exciting to say the least. The score has been going back and forth through all four quarters. Each team has shown they both deserved to be here today. It has been an amazing game! This packed gymnasium trembles with the cheers from the cheerleaders as well as the fans showing their support.

Jenny Soler is on the court as point guard for the Scarlets after that last time out. This is not her usual position. She's usually playing forward or center but she's a very versatile player and is used where ever the team needs her. Her leadership abilities show as she calls the play while she dribbles down the court.

Wait!

What happened?

There's been a HUGE gasp from the crowd. All the cheering stopped. The play on the court has stopped. I'm not sure why.

Was there sweat on the court? No.

They just cleaned the court during the last time out. No one was near her. She wasn't pushed. Her sneakers are tied so she didn't trip over her laces.

Good thing she has those knee pads on, but we still don't know why she fell. We don't know what caused her to fall.

Wait, just a moment...

This just in from the courtside...

THE MYSTERY

The year 1989.

A junior in high school with a promising future, ranked 5th in her class scholastically and very involved in after school activities including riding on the Volunteer Ambulance Corps as an Emergency Medical Technician (EMT).

She didn't get "in trouble".

She didn't take drugs.

She didn't drink.

She respected her parents and her elders.

She was in the National Honor Society.

She was in the National Art Honor Society.

She was on the Math Team.

She was on the Debate team.

She was on the Prom Committee.

Everything looked like it was out of a fairytale, the ones

that start with "Once upon a time…" and end with "Happily ever after".

She had the perfect life or so it seemed. Something happened. Something just wasn't right. What went wrong? Why did she fall? Stay tuned for more on that right after this…

WEEKS BEFORE

I had a tingling sensation in my left foot that started during basketball practice. I ignored it chalking it up to my sneakers being tied too tight, or the tape around my ankle not put on correctly. That feeling was nothing I told myself - it was invalid.

Then the next day, my right foot started feeling the same way. Again I dismissed it to my sneakers being tied too tight or maybe I was growing again and my sneakers were too small.

It was nothing to be worried about; at least that is what I told myself again. Then within the next couple of days the tingling started traveling up my legs. That is when I said something to my mom.

That was when it started to become *real*. I had to admit to myself and to one of the most important persons in my life something was wrong. These invalid feelings in my feet now started crawling up my legs and I had to tell someone.

I went to my mom one night after basketball practice before going to bed for the night but after all three of my younger brothers were in bed.

"Mom, I have something I need to talk to you about. I have been experiencing this tingling feeling in my feet kinda like when your foot falls asleep and now it's waking up. Well actually it started in my left foot but now it is in both of my feet."

She immediately pulled off my shoes and my socks and felt my feet.

She then said, "Your feet are frozen! They shouldn't feel this cold! When did this start?"

"About a week ago, I ignored it. I didn't think it was anything, but I needed to tell you now because the tingling has started traveling up my legs."

"I don't know what to tell you. If it doesn't hurt I don't know what I could give you to make it go away. Why don't you mention it to your basketball coach tomorrow, maybe he'll have an idea?"

Before approaching my basketball coach with this information, I approached the wrestling coach and asked if I could borrow a set of knee pads.

"Coach, I need to talk with you before we start practice."

"Sure, Jenny, but why do you have wrestling knee pads on?"

"That is what I need to talk to you about. I borrowed these knee pads from the wrestling coach because about a week ago my feet started falling asleep while I was playing on the court, but now the tingling has turned into numbness up to my knees."

"Does it hurt? Are you in pain?"

"No, but since my feet and shins are numb I decided to put on the knee pads so I don't hurt myself."

"Well I'll keep an eye on you during practice and see if I can come up with something."

I participated in practice just as I had been, but now I had those knee pads on and I felt I could "throw" myself after the ball in any attempts to steal with no fear.

My coach watched my playing over the next few days and had the trainer watch me as well. They both noticed my legs didn't appear as strong as they should and with the help of the knee pads I spent a lot of time on the floor. My coach called my mom to come to the gym to pick me up after practice so they could talk.

"Mrs. Soler, I have been watching Jenny during practice and I asked the trainer to watch her as well. We do not know what could be causing this but the first thing I would do is take her to a chiropractor. I can give you the name of the one, one of the other players goes to. The other player went to the chiropractor because she slipped a disc in her spine. Maybe that is what is going on with Jenny."

We called the chiropractor my coach recommended, but the first available appointment wasn't until after the state championship game.

I limped into the chiropractor's office on that first visit, my mom and I told him about all the strange things I had been experiencing and about falling down during that game. He said the first thing he needed to do was to take an x-ray of my spine.

Remember this as you read these next words,

(I was 16 years old, 5 feet 8 inches tall, weighed 145 pounds and very athletic...)

The chiropractor came back with the x-ray and said, "I knew you said you were only sixteen, but your pelvis is in the position of a woman who had experienced multiple births, and you are carrying too much weight for your spine."

My mom responded in a joking manner, "Are you sure you're not looking at my x-ray? I'm the one who has given birth to 4 children and am truly the one who is overweight."

I only weighed 145 pounds at 5'8" in height. The last thing that should be said to a 16 year old girl who is scared and doesn't know what is happening to her body is she is FAT!

I lost 5 pounds in 5 days and I also lost my ability to walk on my own by the end of those 5 days. I saw that chiropractor everyday for those 5 days and everyday my ability to even wiggle my toes was less and less. Finally on that fifth day; the chiropractor watched as I slowly hobbled dragging my feet into his office with my mom as a human crutch.

He told us he wasn't going to adjust my spine that day but he wanted to do something different. He assisted me up onto the examining table because I couldn't lift my legs on my own. He then asked me to close my eyes as my mom watched trying to hold back the tears. He told me to let him know when I felt him touch me.

After what seemed like 10 minutes, I felt him, FINALLY, touch my shoulder. I opened my eyes to see my mom holding her face in her hands no longer able to hold back the tears and my legs covered with red spots that were put there by the sharp spur-like instrument the doctor had been using to test my ability to sense touch.

I can't even begin to explain all the thoughts that were going through my mind when I saw all those red spots all over my legs. My legs looked like they do after I have had them waxed. They looked like someone was playing connect the dots on my legs, only they hadn't drawn the lines yet. Then feeling how sharp that spur-like instrument actually was as he ran the same instrument over my hands and arms. He only had to touch me once on my arm to know I had lost all "sense of feeling" below my knees and that loss was quickly traveling up both my legs.

I already knew I couldn't walk without assistance, what else could go wrong? What was happening to me? Why was this happening to me?

At this point I got really scared! The chiropractor asked my mom to step out of the room with him. He felt that whatever was happening to me, he couldn't talk about in front of me! I was too young to know!

When my mom returned to the room where I was still on the examining table with my "dead" feet dangling over the edge of the treatment table waiting for her help to put my shoes back on and those red spots seemingly getting bigger. She told me we had to go to the Emergency Room (ER) to meet up with some "specialists".

I don't know if the red spots really were getting bigger or if it was just what I could see through the tears in my eyes.

Wait, I thought we were seeing a specialist, but I was getting worse not better! I lost 5 pounds that week because he said I was fat.

Didn't that help?

I did what I was supposed to do, didn't I?

What was going on? I just played in a state championship game last Saturday!

I don't take drugs!

I don't drink!

I didn't get hit by a car!

I didn't fall out of a tree!

Why can't I feel my legs?

What did I do wrong?

Why me?

THE SPECIALISTS

O ff to the ER to meet with "The Specialists".

This time my mom went in without me to get a wheelchair because I was getting tired from dragging my feet. My legs felt like I had a 2 ton ball and chain attached to each one of my ankles. That must be when she used a phone to call my father.

I rode a wheelchair into the ER I visited often, not as a patient but as an EMT. As I sat waiting while my mom filled out the paperwork. I rolled closer to the patient treatment area waiting to see what was going to happen next. I saw other people from the ambulance squad I volunteered at bringing in a patient and I saw people from the EMT classes I attended going in and out of the ER also bringing in more patients, all of them wondering why I was there and in a wheelchair.

It is amazing how different an Emergency Room(ER) seems from the point of view of a patient than from a nurse, a doctor or even a medic/EMT who disembarks the patients from the ambulances. I couldn't just go through the doors and into the area I would take my patient to after I helped to unload them from the ambulance just as I was seeing happen before my eyes as I waited. With the use of a "bed" referred to as a gurney I would assist my fellow medics first in using teamwork to lift the patient out of the ambulance and then with the push of a button drop the wheels to then escort/roll the patient into the ER. The Medics/EMTs including myself would have asked all the questions of the patient necessary to get the proper medical treatment for the patient and then our job was to inform the nurse on duty of all the information we had collected.

There were no medics asking me the questions before I entered the ER this time. The doctors who requested I meet them there hadn't arrived yet. Nurses not knowing why I was there kept asking the usual questions to figure out what they should do with me to try and make me feel comfortable.

"What brings you to the ER on a Friday evening? What is your chief complaint? Were you involved in an accident? Did you fall?" All the same questions I was asking myself on the car ride there.

I gave them the same answers I was telling myself. "I don't know why I'm at an ER on a Friday night. I should be hanging out with my friends. No, I

wasn't in an accident. No, I didn't fall. I just can't
feel my legs and I don't know why!"

I was moved from the wheelchair I was sitting in, onto a gurney
that had been dropped slightly lower than the seat of the wheelchair.
One nurse grabbed my legs while I used my upper body strength
to slide the rest of the way holding onto another nurse then the
nurses picked up the gurney and dropped the wheels. I was sitting
partially inclined like I was in the wheelchair so I could see what
was going on around me and I could talk to some of my EMT
friends as they started packing up their gear as well as cleaning off
their gurney. I waited for "The Specialists".

"The Specialists" had arrived and so did my dad. They only
talked to my mom and dad, not to me. My parents told me when
"The Specialists" left they wanted to do a spinal tap to see if I
might have a tumor in my spine causing the numbness because the
chiropractor had told them I didn't have any slipped or herniated
disks. My parents told me the doctors did not want to scare or
alarm me so they only spoke to my parents.

The doctors didn't want to alarm me!
They didn't want to scare me?!?
Didn't they realize I was already scared?!
I was running suicide drills up and down the basketball court

with my teammates just a week ago! Now I couldn't even feel the
socks on my feet!

I couldn't feel if my feet were WARM or COLD!

I must have fooled them all. They couldn't see all the fear I was
feeling because I just kept smiling. I joked with the nurses. I kidded
with my EMT friends. I spoke nicely with the orderlies.

Into the radiology wing of the hospital for the spinal tap I went.

No one told me what a spinal tap was. I thought I was just going to
get another x-ray.

Then the x-ray tech came over to me and asked if I could
be pregnant.

Pregnant, I'm still a virgin!

Then she explained she would be shooting a dye into my spine to
be able to see the spinal cord more clearly. She asked me to roll on
my side and try not to jump when she stuck me with the needle.

It was probably a good thing I didn't see the needle. I was afraid of
needles. I didn't like getting stuck with them even for vaccines.

I was returned back to my gurney after the spinal tap was complete
that was still in the inclined position which was fine by me that way
I could see what was going on around me in the ER.

"The Specialists" told my parents out of my
earshot, "We have good news and bad news. We
want to keep your daughter in the hospital for

THE SPECIALISTS ※ 19

observation. The good news is she doesn't have any slipped or herniated discs. Some more good news is she doesn't have anything causing pressure on her spinal cord. Even more good news is she has no tumors, cancerous or not.

The bad news is we don't have any ideas just yet on what could be causing her numbness. We need to consult with some of our other colleagues that won't be available until the next day being it is already late Friday night."

My parents agreed and had me admitted. I was placed in the pediatric ward because I was only 16. I think this influenced how the doctors treated me. They probably felt I was too young to understand or comprehend what was happening, so they would never speak in front of me. They always spoke with my parents out of my earshot. They didn't know I already lost a patient to suicide and I also helped to rescue a friend after a motorcycle accident as an EMT on the ambulance corps. They didn't see how mature I really was. They only saw 16 years old on my chart and I was located in the pediatric wing.

I was put in a room by myself and to avoid personal accidents, because I couldn't walk on my own, the doctors had a catheter, a thin flexible tube that is inserted into a part of the body to drain away fluid, attached to a collection bag put in place. My parents had to get home for my three younger brothers. I understood this, but I was still scared.

I didn't know what was happening. I didn't want to be alone. I was scared! I prayed all night. I asked God for strength. I asked God for an answer about what was happening to me. I asked God for forgiveness for everything, for my thoughts, for my actions, for not telling my mom sooner. Was I that bad? Was I being punished?

I did what I was supposed to do, didn't I?

I was only 16!

I just played in a state championship game last Saturday!

I didn't take drugs!

I didn't drink!

I didn't get hit by a car!

I didn't fall out of a tree!

Why can't I feel my legs?

What did I do wrong?

ONLY 20%

The next morning during hospital rounds I met the doctors that admitted me. They were neurologists, the specialists that only dealt with nerves.

My parents were also there when the doctors, only two out of the three that were there the night before, came to examine me. One doctor took charge of the examination as the other watched.

He started the typical neurological examination. He started with the upper body. He held up his pointer finger and then asked me to touch his finger with mine and then touch my nose which I could do with no problem. Then he held up three of his fingers and asked me to squeeze his fingers to test my grip; the doctor was amazed to feel how tight my grip actually was. He asked me to shrug my shoulders with him pushing down on them, which again was no problem. He asked me to follow his finger with my eyes; first side to side then up and down. No problems there. Then he took out a safety pin and tested my sense of touch on my arms. He first touched my arm near my elbow, it was sharp. Then he touched the backs of my hands, it was still equally sharp.

That was when he started to test my lower body. He at first asked me to lift my legs one at a time. I couldn't. He asked me to wiggle my toes. I couldn't. Then with my eyes closed he asked me to respond to him touching my shins. Silent tears started to run down my cheeks wondering when he was going to start. I couldn't feel him. He used the same safety pin he used on my arms and tried touching my thighs. He asked me to open my eyes and I watched as he touched my legs with the pin. I saw him try pushing harder with the pin. I didn't feel it. I couldn't feel it! He asked me to roll on my side to test my backside. He told me he was going to test my lower legs first.

It seemed like forever, was he ever going to start?

Then I felt the pin on my lower back above my buttocks to which I responded, "Ouch!"

That was when the doctors told me to relax and asked my parents to step out into the hallway. At first I could see them standing outside my door. I think one of the doctors noticed I was watching then asked my parents to go down the hall where they could all sit down and talk. I know this because my mom told me they would be right back.

Where were they going? Why wouldn't they tell ME what was going on? Didn't I deserve to hear what was going on with MY body?

My parents returned in what seemed to me like an eternity later. It seemed a lot longer than it took for me to finally feel that pin stick in my back. I heard their voices in the hall, I heard the emotions in my mom's words, I heard the anger in my dad's voice, but I couldn't make out what they were saying. I couldn't understand the words I could make out. They stayed in the hall a little longer, probably to put on a good show for me.

My parents finally came back into the room, neither of them with positive looks on their faces, both of them wondering if they should tell me what the neurologists told them in the room down the hall. Both of them wondering if what they had heard come out of the mouths of "The Specialists" was really true. My mom couldn't look at me without crying. My dad didn't know what to think never mind what to say. They were both in shock.

Before they could say a word the nurse came in to tell me the doctor left orders to start an IV drip. I turned my face away as she put the needle in my left wrist. She told me it was a heparin lock and it would be in place for a few days so they wouldn't have to stick me every day. With the heparin lock in place they could give me my medicine and take blood samples without torturing me with needles everyday. That was when my parents finally said something. They said what the doctors had told them was a little disturbing. They said they told the doctors to go ahead with the treatment the doctors felt was the only thing that could be done.

The neurologists gave my parents this disturbing news. They told my parents they gave me, the very athletic daughter, the one who is very involved in after school activities, the one who helps others by being on the volunteer ambulance corps, the oldest of four children, an 80% chance of NEVER reusing my legs again.

"The Specialists" gave me an 80% chance I would NEVER use my legs again! "The Specialists" said I would be attached to a catheter and collection bag until further notice. They said I would be using a wheelchair to get around and be a paraplegic.

My parents scared and horrified by this news put up a fight, they asked for something, anything to try and improve my chances of getting out of that bed. The doctors said they had one option to offer my parents. They said this option came with risks but if it was going to work it would work right away.

My parents still weren't sure how to tell me what this heparin line placed in my arm was actually going to be used for. Finally my mom just came out and said it. She said I would be on an IV drip of Solumedrol for a few days. She said I would have side effects but this was my only hope of regaining the use of my legs.

Solumedrol – what is Solumedrol? What are these side effects?

Well I found out what these side effects were. The nurse gave me a list.

- Acne – *ok – I already have that – nothing new there*

- Nausea – *Well I may feel like I might throw up*

- Vomiting – *ok self explanatory*

- Changes in appetite – *ok I just lost 5 lbs. in one week, can't be that bad*

- Diarrhea – *well that's better than constipation*

- Constipation – *Wait, how can I have both?*

- Heartburn – *I can take something for that, right?*

- Headache – *I can take something for that, that I know*

- Restlessness – *well, I already am experiencing that*

- Difficulty sleeping – *duh – already experiencing that*

- Sweating – *I'm an athlete, I know sweat*

- Changes in eyesight – *I have 20/20 vision, no worries there*

- Metal taste in mouth – *ok that sounds gross*

- Mood swings - *?????*

Hey wait a minute, these sound like the side effects I learned about in health class.

I remember them from the lesson on why taking steroids is bad for you!
I KNOW I SHOULDN'T TAKE STEROIDS!

"Nurse, are they giving me steroids? Is this really my only hope?"

In came the second nurse with the bag of "drugs"! I had no choice if I wanted to feel my feet again I had to try something. My mom told me about the 80/20 figures the doctors told them about.

I told my mom, "I'll take that 20 Percent and I **WILL** walk again!"

After about three days of receiving 1000mg of Solumedrol each day. My vision got blurry, food tasted like metal, but I wanted to eat all of it and then some, I didn't feel nauseous, I was moody and I wasn't sleeping instead I was praying and asking God for strength and asking God to let me feel my feet again. Friends came to visit me, I thanked them for the flowers, but all I wanted was food!!!

The doctors visited me during rounds every morning, and every morning there was no change except on day number three. On day number three, I could wiggle my big toe!

On day number four with my parents present, I could wiggle my toe! I could wiggle all my toes! That was when the doctors asked my parents to step outside of the room again. Again outside of my earshot!

Hey I'm the one who took your 20% and took the steroids I didn't want to. Why won't you talk to me? I'm the one you keep sticking with the pins. I'm the one you keep dragging that thing up the bottom of my feet. Why won't you talk to me?

My parents went down the hall with the doctors to talk in private.

After a daily dose of fewer steroids, I was being weaned off of them because of the high dose I had been given at the start. They took out the catheter because I was allowed to "walk" to the bathroom. I was being sent to physical therapy to relearn how to walk and to regain my ability to balance without help. By the time I was ready to be discharged from the hospital, I was walking back and forth from my room to the nurses' station with no assistance!

My last visit from the doctors on the morning of my discharge which was 2 weeks from when I was originally admitted, was a positive one, at least I thought so. I showed them I took the 20% they gave me and I viewed it in a positive way.

I could walk! I could feel! I showed them!

They asked my parents to step out of the room again.

I went home with my parents with a prescription in hand to continue the taper of the steroids through oral prednisone. They did not put any restrictions on me except to limit my use of stairs and no gym class for now. They told me to go back to my life and to go back to school just make sure I took my meds.

I went home to sleep in MY bed. You know the flat mattress, the "normal" kind that doesn't incline like the hospital bed. I had been lying and sleeping in the incline position since they put that needle in my back 2 weeks earlier; no one ever said I should have been laying flat on my back. I thought those headaches were from the steroids, not from me being inclined after a spinal tap.

Well I took my steroids. I took my heartburn medicine. I took Tylenol to cope with the headaches. I even took another medicine for the gas pressure I felt under my lungs and in my stomach. (*No one mentioned that one.*) And I ate! I ate everything!

THE DAY I CAME HOME FROM THE HOSPITAL.

"BACK TO NORMAL"

Back to school I went with "chipmunk cheeks" (another side effect) and visited the attendance office. I told the teacher in charge of attendance of my restriction of not going up and down stairs. She told me no problem I could use the school's elevator.

I became Miss Popular with that idea. I could leave class early. I could be late for the next class and I could take a friend for assistance.

Oh yeah, let me tell you a little about the building my high school was in. The building is a perfect square with two floors. I had the perfect schedule, the perfect schedule if I was using the stairs. My classes were right above and below each other from one hour to the next but they were on the opposite corner from the elevator.

I started the day at the elevator waiting, in a standing position, waiting for someone with a key for the elevator. I had to get to the second floor because that's where my locker was. I had to find a friend to assist me with all my books. I had all of them because I had been out of school for over two weeks. I got to my locker with all my books, but my first class was again on the opposite corner from where the elevator was, but on the first floor. So there I was, walking twice as far as I had been walking to get to the elevator to then go back to the opposite side of the building to get to my class that was right below my homeroom classroom that I had just left. I did all of this to avoid the stairs. I had to avoid the stairs because the doctors were afraid I might fall. This was the case for my entire schedule.

I did it! I made it through the first day back at school. I was welcomed back by the teachers. I was welcomed back by all my friends. I was even welcomed back by people I didn't know. I was asked questions. I was asked all sorts of questions. But the main question, the one question I didn't have an answer to was what was the reason for my fall in that game?

I could tell them I had a needle in my arm. I could even show them the band aids. I could tell them I can walk with no problem. I could show them that. I could tell them about the physical therapy sessions. I could even display some of the balancing "drills". I could tell them about all the medicine I had taken and even tell them about the ones I was still taking.

But I couldn't answer that question. I couldn't answer, why? I couldn't answer the question that was on everyone's mind including my own. I couldn't say what the reason was. I couldn't say why because I didn't know. Being asked these questions all day long started making me angry. Not at the people asking but at the doctors for not telling me. At the doctors for not telling me directly what their suspicions were.

I went home that afternoon from school. I walked upstairs to my bedroom to lie down and rest. I walked upstairs to be alone and to cry and be angry and to ask God again, why me? Why can't I answer that question? Why don't I know what the answer is?

DOZED OFF

Suddenly I woke up on top of my bedspread wearing the same clothes I wore to school the previous day. It was night. All the lights were out in the house. The only light that was on was the street light outside my bedroom window. I was uncomfortable on my flat bed so I walked downstairs to try to find a way to get comfortable on the couch.

I wasn't able to sleep comfortably in my flat bed because I got used to sleeping on the inclined bed in the hospital. No one told me I wouldn't be able to sleep with my legs straight while I was on my back. No one told me the headaches I was having was from the spinal tap not just the steroids.

I woke up. Not because it was time to get up for the morning, I woke up because the legs that only weeks before couldn't feel the socks I was wearing, were now filled with pain, mild pain at first. Then gradually like it happened only weeks before but in the opposite direction, my knees that were not giving me trouble before now, felt like daggers were being shoved underneath my knee caps. The pain kept building and building. The more I tried to ignore it, the stronger the pain felt.

This extreme pain I was feeling made me actually ask for the paralysis back again. I said the words out loud. I screamed in agony. I tried putting pressure on my knees. I tried rocking back and forth on my knees both on the carpet and on the bare floor. I woke up the whole house with my screams and cries of begging for the numbness to return and asking for a reason why this was happening to me, again. Why was I in so much pain?

My mom came downstairs followed by my dad to see what all the yelling was about. She couldn't do anything for me, Mommy's kisses only worked for my little brothers. There was nothing she could do. There was nothing anyone could do. It was the middle of the night. We had to wait until morning. We had to wait for the Specialists to be available. It wasn't life or death; at least that is what the answering service told my parents.

"BUT, IT IS LIFE OR DEATH!!! IT IS MY LIFE! SOMEONE OR SOMETHING TOOK IT AWAY FROM ME! AND IF SOMEONE DOESN'T TAKE THIS PAIN AWAY, I'M GOING TO KILL MYSELF! I WOULD

RATHER BE PARALYZED!" I screamed when I heard my mom repeating what the person on the phone had said to her.

My mom grabbed me and tried to calm me down. She tried to find something stronger than what I had been taking for my headaches. She put heating pads on my knees. She put ice packs on my knees. Finally I think I just passed out again due to sheer exhaustion. Probably that and my legs were frozen from the ice packs making them feel paralyzed.

When I woke up on the floor of the living room around 9 am, my mom told me she had sent two of my brothers to school and the youngest went to my aunt's house. She was able to get in touch with the Specialists who told her to bring me back to the Emergency Room.

So I got changed and tried to make myself presentable and back to the hospital we went. After examining me and seeing I was extremely sensitive to their touch even without a pin, they had come to the conclusion I was weaned off the steroids too quickly.

I explained to them all the walking I had done the day before just to get to class and avoid the stairs. I described the pain in my legs that had only slightly subsided by now because my legs were feeling numb again probably due to the exhaustion I was still feeling or they were still frozen from the ice packs.

They sent me home with more prescriptions. One was for a higher dose of steroids. One was for prescription strength ibuprofen I was to take three times a day. One was for Zantac to keep the acids in my stomach down.

Now I had more prescriptions. I had prescriptions to combat the side effects of the other prescriptions.

I also asked for a script to use a wheelchair. Not because I couldn't walk, just so I didn't have to walk so much to get to the elevator so I could return to my "semi-normal" life. The doctors agreed but still didn't tell me what they were thinking was wrong with me.

THE REASON

I confronted my parents on the car ride home. I finally asked them to tell me what the doctors were telling them outside of my earshot. I knew my parents knew more than what they were telling me. I knew they were holding something back.

When we got home, I think all my begging and pleading got to my parents. They decided to sit down with me and tell me what the doctors had been telling them. My mom and dad had said they were arguing whether or not to tell me what the doctors had convinced them NOT to tell me.

My parents felt I was old enough and mature enough to handle what the doctors had been telling them.

They handed me a pamphlet.

This pamphlet had two big red letters on it at the top.
These two letters stood for the *thing* the doctors said *could* be

what was causing all my problems. They said because of my age, the doctors didn't want to tell me directly. The doctors didn't want to impede my recovery or stigmatize me. They didn't think I would be able to handle it.

The doctors *couldn't* confirm it, so they told my parents not to scare me. There were no tests only judgments based on past experiences. Throughout my short medical history and my family's medical history there was nothing like this that had happened before and I was so young, only 16, their theory *couldn't* be right.

I stared at the pamphlet.

I stared at the cover.

I was afraid to open it.

Was this the answer?

Was this the reason?

Was this really what was wrong with me?

Was this pamphlet going to give me the answer?

Is it what I had been praying for?

PHASE II

THE JOURNEYS
OF DENIAL

OUT OF
MY EARSHOT

My parents finally agreed to tell me what "The Specialists" were telling them out of my earshot.

"Remember when I told you about the steroids they were going to be giving you? Well that was when they told us you would be a paraplegic for the rest of your life," my mom said.

"That was when I started to put up a fight. I told them there had to be something they could try. We didn't want to give you the steroids but that was the only thing they could offer you," my dad said.

"The doctors told us steroids were the only choice they could offer. They said if you didn't respond to them you would not get out of that bed," my mom said with tears in her eyes.

"The doctors mentioned they had a theory but you didn't fit the profile of their theory. That was when they gave us that pamphlet," added my mom.

"Your mother told the doctors all the details about the family's history and nothing added up to their theory," my dad said. "You know they asked us if we ever heard of this before. And I said Multiple, what? I can't even say that and I speak two languages!"

"Then when you started getting better and we were all just so happy that our decision to have to start the steroids was not a bad one, we just wanted to keep celebrating!" cried my mom. "The doctors even told us to forget about the pamphlet. They told us this episode might just be a fluke and to keep celebrating. They said to keep celebrating because you are too young to even consider it especially because you didn't fit the profile. They said you could go your entire life and this incident could be just a memory."

"I WILL DANCE"

I was finally ready to find out more about this journey, I opened the pamphlet after staring at those two red letters for at least an hour. It said MS, short for Multiple Sclerosis, is a chronic disease of the Central Nervous System, CNS.

Oh great, more letters!

It said there is no test to confirm the diagnosis.

So they are not sure. They can't prove it!

It said early signs of the disease are difficulty with vision.

I have perfect vision and have always had perfect vision.

It said it affects people in their late twenties and early thirties.

Hey, I'm only 16! No wonder they told my parents to forget about it. Because I am better and I really don't fit the profile.

I got back to my "normal" 16 year old life. I continued to help out with the Prom committee. I attended my classes as usual but this time I was in a wheelchair, not because I couldn't walk, but because I didn't want to walk so much. The doctors insisted I continue to avoid the stairs. I rode in the wheelchair I borrowed from the ambulance corps I volunteered at. I was smiling and happy. I was <u>HAPPY</u> to be back to my "normal" life.

One day my happiness and accomplishments were challenged. One moment that has survived in my memory banks for over 18 years, was when a "smart" (*I put that in quotes to stress the next statement*) sophomore who was in my junior level math class questioned how I could come to school in a wheelchair.

She said, "I would be so embarrassed to be seen in a wheelchair!"

I thought to myself and may have vocalized some of these thoughts as well. I was paralyzed, but my brain still works and my legs do, too! Just to let you know, I will be dancing at the prom.

Dance I did! I danced wearing 3 inch heals, no wheelchair, no crutches. No sign of paralysis.

ME AT MY JUNIOR PROM WEARING 3 INCH HEALS!

THANKFULNESS

While I was going through my "journey" there was another Jen in my town going through a "journey" of her own. She was younger than I. Her "journey" had another name; her "journey's" name was Cancer. I know and remember this most profoundly because her family and friends held several benefit events almost every month during the same time as I was learning about what my "journey" was called.

I was living in a small town in New Jersey and all that was in the newspapers and on the local news and on the lips of the local rumor mills was this girl named Jennifer with Cancer. I don't really remember Jennifer's full name. In the social circles of this little town all you had to say was, "Did you hear about the latest concert for that girl with Cancer?" Everyone knew about the girl with cancer. I knew about the girl with cancer. I felt sorry for the girl with cancer. Because I wasn't the girl with cancer and I didn't want to be the girl with anything else. I just wanted to be Jenny. I wanted to be the girl who did a great job on planning the prom. I wanted to be the girl on the Honor Society who worked at the local pizza parlor. I wanted to be the helpful girl with a lot of friends who rode on the volunteer ambulance corps. I did not want to be the girl everybody knew because they felt sorry for her. *(P.S. Jen, if you are reading this, I hope you are doing fine!)*

After reading that pamphlet and everything else I could get my hands on that had to do with MS, I decided I didn't have it and no one else was going to hear those two letters associated with my name! I didn't feel sorry for me, not anymore. I didn't question God anymore, I thanked him. I thanked him for giving me the strength to overcome. I again remember the 20% the doctors gave me and what I did with God's assistance. I was walking, dancing, running and smiling!

Whenever anyone would ask about that game, or what had happened to me, I would just shrug my shoulders and say the doctors didn't know. I would say, "It doesn't matter, not anymore. I'm not in the hospital. I just have to finish weaning off the medicine. I'm walking again and, yes, I will be playing basketball next season!"

I spent that summer working out. I trained on the basketball court. I ran killer drills. I started lifting weights. I did leg presses of my current body weight of 160 lbs. *(I told you, I ate everything!)* I rode my bicycle throughout town and to several other nearby towns. I became a skate guard at the roller rink. I returned that wheelchair to the ambulance corps on my first night back on active duty. I did everything I could from a standing position. I took that 20% and I "ran" with it, literally. Those two letters weren't what I had, and I was going to prove it to myself and everyone else!

LITTLE BROTHERS

It was fall, time to go back to school. For my baby brother, the youngest of the three, he was going to school full time for the first time. He was starting first grade. He was so cute, wearing his little uniform. I was so proud of him. He started learning how to count and to say his ABC's. He even learned how to write his ABC's including his initials.

My little baby brother enjoyed writing his initials. He enjoyed writing them so much, he wrote them everywhere. He wrote them on the newspaper. He wrote them on the wall. He wrote them on everything including my notebooks. If there was a writing implement, he wrote his initials. I bet you are wondering what this has to do with me. Well, my baby brother's initials are MS. So it was a little too hard NOT to think about those two innocent letters.

I started my senior year, no wheelchair. Wearing high heals every chance I could. No signs of paralysis. I used the stairs just like everyone else. I had my "normal" life back again.

Then, it was hay fever season, or maybe it was one of the colds my little brothers brought home from school, no matter, I was sick with a head cold. I was sniffling and coughing and I had headaches. I was done with the steroids. I had been done with the steroids for several months by this time. Most of the side effects had dwindled and there were no signs I couldn't walk less than 6 months ago, but now I have a "normal" head cold.

The sniffling subsided. The coughing ended. Now, I had an itch in my ear. I'm not sure if it was an itch or if I had an ear ache. I told my mom my ear felt weird. I had just turned 17 in September and I had been granted a new sense of freedom, my driver's license. I was questioning if I should be seen by a pediatrician because I was older now, but I went anyway.

The Pediatrician even questioned why I was in to see him because of my age. He still examined me, but wasn't sure what was wrong. He didn't see any infection in my ear. He sent me to a "Specialist". This "specialist" wasn't a neurologist; this "specialist" was an ENT, not an EMT, which I was. He was an ENT, an Ear, Nose and Throat Doctor. The ENT doctor started this visit with a preliminary hearing test. He told me they would put me in a sound proof booth with head phones on and I was to raise my hand on the side I heard a sound.

That sounds pretty easy. The nurse used to do that to me in school every year.

So, into the booth I went. Boop, booooop, bip. High and low. Sounds were traveling from one ear to the next. Then some sounds were only in one ear but not the other. The doctor called me out of the booth. He said my hearing was not good. He said I was on the verge of deafness on one side.

This can't be. I just had a cold. I must just be stuffy. A head cold couldn't make me deaf, could it?

My mom and I informed the doctor of the paralysis I experienced 6 months earlier. He took this into account and said he didn't want to label it - yet. He wanted to try an antibiotic first. Off we went to the pharmacy with prescription in hand with the hope this deafness was what the doctor said it might be. He said he wanted to try the antibiotic for a week and recheck my hearing. He said if my hearing improved then it was just an infection stuck behind the eardrum and the antibiotic would take care of it.

I started taking the antibiotic. I went to school as usual, but by this time I was having more difficulties hearing on the right side. I would sit in class with my head turned so my left ear was closer to where the teacher was teaching from. I told my friends when they walked with me down the hall in between classes to make sure they were on my left side. I attempted to try to learn how to read lips which is a lot harder than it looks.

One day while walking between classes, wearing high healed boots, because I could, my friend, who under normal circumstances was shorter than me but on this occasion was an additional 3 inches shorter was talking to me. I accidentally dropped my books and we both stooped over to pick them up. He looked at me and asked why I didn't answer his question. That was when I realized he was walking on my right side and I hadn't heard a word he said.

It was the day of my follow up appointment with the ENT doctor. My mom and I arrived at the doctor's office and after all of the niceties, I found myself where I expected to be in the sound booth with the headset on.

"Boop",

Pause

"Beep",

Pause

"Bip",

Pause

The door to the booth opened. The doctor did not look happy. He actually looked a little worried, as worried as a doctor is allowed to look when he has to deliver bad news. His bad news was I didn't respond to any sounds on the right side at all. He looked worried but a little hopeful. He said all was not lost. He said he wanted to try one other prescription before he diagnosed me with complete deafness. He wanted to try some oral steroids.

Not again! I just finished the taper. I don't have the side effects anymore! I don't want that metal taste in my mouth again! I just started enjoying the taste of food! I finally had control of my mood swings.

The ENT doctor sympathized with me after seeing the disappointing look on my face. He said let's try it for a week at a low dose and then he would retest my hearing. He said if there is no improvement then he would have no choice but to say I lost my hearing on the right side.

"Let's think positive," he said, "we aren't out of the woods yet. Let's try to stay positive."

Let's stay Positive, that's easy for him to say. He isn't the one taking the steroids. He wasn't the one who just regained the use of her legs. But I will take the steroids! I want to be able to hear again.

Take the steroids, I did! Sixty milligrams of Deltazone is what I took for a week. One week later I returned to the ENT doctor with a big smile on my face. That smile was because I didn't have to tell my friends to walk on my left. I could hear the person on the other end of the phone line no matter what ear I had it on. I was smiling because the doctor was NOT going to say I was deaf.

Into the sound proof booth I went and put on the headset.

"Boop".

"Boop".

"Beep".

"Beep".

"Bip".

"Bip".

I did it! I heard them all!

The doctor opened the door to the booth and asked me to come out. I was smiling, a big smile, but the doctor had that familiar look. It was similar to one I had seen before. It was NOT similar to mine but similar to the one he had the week before. The same look most doctors have just before they are about to deliver bad news and deliver bad news he did.

He asked me and my mom to go and sit in his office so we could talk. As we waited for the doctor to return, so many thoughts went through my head as I'm sure went through my mom's.

I can hear!

I'm not deaf!

So, why does the doctor look sad?

The doctor came into the office with my file under his arm and he sat behind his desk. He placed my file closed in front of him on his desk. He then placed his hand on my file and started talking about the things in my file. He started saying he had talked with the neurologists we had told him I had seen 6 months earlier. He told us of the conversations he had with them.

Then he said with a sigh as I recall it, "I hate to be the one to tell you this, but based on your reaction to the steroids and the regaining of your hearing as well as your overcoming of paralysis 6 months earlier, you must have MS."

NO! He can't be right. There is no way to prove it for sure!

I questioned his diagnosis. I stated I was only 17! The pamphlet said it doesn't affect people until they are in their late 20's.

The doctor agreed the evidence was shaky. He said usually the first sign of MS is blindness. That deafness is very rare in MS. He told us to go home and not to worry about it. Not to worry about it because I was only 17 and I had my whole life to live.

We went home. The car ride was the quietest one I had ever been on. I don't even remember hearing the noise from the engine or the radio. The only sounds I kept hearing was the sound of the doctor's voice saying over and over again, "You have MS. You have MS. You have MS."

*No, it can't be true! It isn't true, I'm only 17! I'm NOT blind! I'm
not even deaf anymore. He wasn't even sure. I know I don't have it!*

I got home. I saw my youngest brother's initials on my notebook
that I left on the table. I saw his initials in big bold letters hanging
on the refrigerator. I ran to my room. On the way to my room
was my two littlest brothers' room, I looked at the closed door that
bore both of their initials. The paper on the top had my youngest
brother's initials. The paper on the bottom had my other brother's
initials. Those two pieces of paper expressed the thoughts that were
in my head precisely!

I'M NOT A "JERRY'S KID"

I went through the rest of my senior year of high school like every other kid my age. No signs of paralysis. I could hear everything. Whenever anyone would ask what had happened, I would just say the doctors didn't know. I did however tell my closest friends. I told them the doctors called it Multiple Something or other. I told them I was still the same person I was before any of this started.

I was dating a friend of mine, nothing serious. We were just each others date whenever we would hang out with big groups of friends. He was also one of the friends I told about the two letters.

One day I was sitting at the dining room table of his mom's house. He was upstairs getting ready to go out. We were meeting a bunch of friends to hang out, probably to go get ice cream or to go to a movie. His mom was looking at me. She was looking at me with this look of concern on her face. She was looking at me like something was wrong. I felt a chill in the air.

Finally I said something. I asked her if there *was* something wrong. She looked at me in surprise and told me her son had told her.

Told her what? What did he tell her? Did he tell her I was sick?

"What did he tell you?" I asked. She said her son told her what I had told him but she didn't understand because I looked so good. She said I didn't look sick. She didn't understand why I didn't have a cane or any other devices on my legs. She said you don't look like one of those kids on that telethon. She said you don't look like one of "Jerry's kids"!

That was a memorable moment! Sitting in the dining room of a friend and being confronted with the fear there may be others who would look at me like she did.

No, I'm not sick. I don't want to talk about it, but…

I explained what little I knew about MS to my friend's mom and I told her she didn't have to worry. I wasn't a "Jerry's Kid". "Jerry's Kids" suffered with MD, Muscular Dystrophy, I was told I *might* have Multiple Sclerosis but it wasn't definite and MS is not contagious.

I was still denying it. It didn't matter. I was going away to college and Rob was just a friend not someone I was serious about.

MY NEW LIFE

It was the fall of 1990. I was a freshman in college but not just any college. I wasn't going to take it easy on myself, after all the doctors only gave me a 20% chance of walking again and I refused to believe the other doctor's conclusion. So I went to one of the most difficult colleges to get into in New Jersey. I went to Stevens Institute of Technology, in Hoboken, NJ. I wanted the full college experience so I lived on campus, even though the school was only 20 minutes from my house.

Freshman year started off well. It was a new beginning for me. No one in Hoboken knew I had been in a wheelchair. No one in Hoboken knew I had been deaf. And I didn't have to tell them. I chose not to tell anyone.

Then one night in November, I was awoken by this excruciating pain in my abdomen. I didn't know what to do, I contacted a friend on campus, who contacted campus security who took me and my friend to the hospital.

When we got there, I asked my friend to get me a wheelchair because the pain was so intense I lost the feeling in my legs. The intake nurse told me I had to walk into the Emergency Room. I told her I couldn't. I told her I couldn't feel my legs enough to walk on my own. I had to tell her and my friend that I had only been walking for a little over a year. That the doctors had suspected MS was the cause, but they weren't sure. She looked at me in dismay and confusion. She, the nurse, was confused. She insisted I walk into the ER. After many tears and still in extreme pain, I walked holding on to my friend and I whispered into his ear, "Please, call my parents!"

I waited for what felt like an eternity similar to the time I waited for the doctor to touch me almost a year before. It was a really long time before anyone came back to see what was wrong. By this time the pain had radiated throughout my body, I couldn't even tell them where the pain was anymore. I was getting angry because I was scared, in pain and they didn't believe what I told them.

I don't think I should be here. They don't even know what MS is forget about what might be causing my pain.

My parents got to my bedside within an hour as we waited for the results of some test. My dad was pacing asking why the doctor hadn't been in to see me yet. I actually got out of my bed and hunched over the nurses desk of the ER to ask them what we were waiting for. The nurse told me the lab was at low staff because of the time of night. Then she said we were actually waiting for the results of a pregnancy test because I couldn't recall when I had my last menstrual period. I returned to my bed. Moments after I said out loud it would only take an E.P.T. test from the drug store 10 minutes, in came a nurse with a wheelchair to take me to x-ray.

"Hooray, I'm not pregnant!" I yelled.

I waited for a long time with the pain getting more intense as the night dragged on. It was so intense even my finger tips were throbbing with pain never mind the numbness in my feet. Finally, the doctor came to my bedside and said I was "F.O.S."

"F.O.S.", what is FOS?

The doctor said I was Full Of S***. Not that they didn't believe me but the x-ray showed that my bowels were full, meaning I was constipated. They gave me some Maalox and sent me on my way.

I spent the entire night in the Emergency Room in pain to be sent home with a bottle of Maalox! Along with instructions to not eat a lot until my bowels were cleared.

We, my parents and me, accepted what the doctor said because he showed us the x-ray. I followed the doctor's instructions as far as my diet was concerned. I went on a liquid diet, not alcoholic drinks after all I was only 18, but I was still getting these excruciating pains so Maalox was my new friend.

My mom scheduled an appointment for me with the MS Gimbel Center in Teaneck, NJ. This appointment was just supposed to be a follow-up to my hospital stays from the previous year. I still refused to believe or admit I had MS. After all I couldn't even pronounce the S word.

When I went to the Center for my visit to meet all the nice people that worked there, my mom and I told the doctor about my frequent visits to the Emergency Room over the previous 8 months and that the doctors in those ERs kept telling me I was "FOS". The neurologist said you definitely have MS because difficulty with bowel movements is common even though you are so young. It usually doesn't happen until later stages of the disease they said. So he made an appointment for me to have a 40 gallon water enema there in the office.

If one has never experienced an enema before, it is a procedure I do NOT recommend! Did I mention I was only 18 years old?

After undergoing that traumatic and embarrassing experience and still not openly admitting I had MS, I went back to college and tried to continue with my "normal" life. I had stopped my liquid dieting and started to eat from the campus cafeteria again. Then one night again about 3 am, after I had a single slice of pizza around 8pm, I was jolted awake by this amazing pain again. It was even more intense than the last time I was told I was F.O.S. I didn't hesitate this time, I got to the hall pay phone because freshmen weren't allowed to have phones in their rooms and cell phones only existed for rich people at that time. I called my mom. My mom brought the Maalox and some fennel seed tea. But there was nothing in my system anymore; I was starting to become dehydrated. I couldn't even keep the Maalox down, never mind the tea.

My mom loaded me in the car and raced me to Holy Name Hospital in Teaneck, assuming they would know what to do, after all that is where the MS Center was and where I had that embarrassing procedure.

I was kept in pain for over 13 hours, even with me begging for morphine, because they wanted to locate the origin of the pain. The doctors really weren't sure what was causing my pain. They took x-rays but my bowels were empty. I was getting weaker and weaker. I couldn't stay awake because I was dehydrated. I was finally admitted with a Urinary Tract Infection.

After admitting me, the doctors tested my digestive system with Nuclear Radii placed in my digestive system that they could view on a TV screen. The radii were followed through my esophagus, down through my stomach, then into my liver and eventually into my small intestine and then my large intestine and finally out through my colon. Wait, it missed an organ! It didn't touch my gall bladder. I learned that in biology in high school, not to mention in my college freshman-year biology class. It was determined I had gall stones. Not little ones either, we are talking marble size stones and one of them was blocking the path to allow it to function properly and thus causing all the pain. All the pain I had been going through for the last 9 months was caused by gall stones, not because I was F.O.S.

Why hadn't anyone looked at the gall bladder before? Gall stones aren't rare!

I voiced these thoughts to the doctors. Their response was I didn't fit the profile not the full profile of 4 F's. The 4F profile stands for Female, Fat, over Forty, and Fair. I only qualified for one of the F's, Female. I wasn't fat. I was only 18 years old and I still had my deep tan from all the hours of life guarding over the summer.

I was kept in this hospital for a week on a liquid diet. The doctor wanted to make my gall bladder "cool" so they could operate. The doctor said my best choice was to have the entire gall bladder removed because once the gall bladder starts forming stones even if they are removed it will continue to make more.

The doctor didn't want to cause another gall bladder attack, even though I begged for food. I convinced the doctor to let me have some crackers with my lunch. That was a mistake. That one little cracker caused a major gall bladder attack. After the nurse found me on the floor by the toilet in the hall restroom, my doctor was called in.

I was then transferred to a hospital in NYC in order to have my "hot", enflamed gall bladder removed. All because I didn't fit the

4 F's, Female, Fat, Forty +, Fair, no one even considered looking at my gall bladder because they all thought this problem was caused by MS and I was so young.

I told them I didn't have that!

NEW LIFE: TAKE 2

I made it through the rest of that year, 1991, without those two letters showing up. I played on my college's women's basketball team.

I even made it through the next year, 1992, and played on my college's women's soccer team.

Then in January 1993, my hands and arms decided to stop cooperating, which made titrating fluids in my chemistry labs or typing reports and homework for my classes a little difficult. Only a couple of months before, I started dating this guy, Chris. Because we had been getting so close, I told him about the two letters that kept following me around. I told him about the previous journeys I had been forced to take. He didn't seem to care about them, he seemed to only care about me, or he really didn't believe those two letters existed for me just like I didn't believe it either.

I couldn't take it anymore; the stiffness in my arms was starting to run down my side, I had to see the doctor. The doctors were concerned I not lose out on school so they put me in the hospital for some IV steroid treatment to try and circumvent this new journey. That guy, the one I was dating, came to visit me in the hospital undergoing my steroid treatment. He wasn't there when I was hooked up to the IV but he did see the thing sticking out of my arm, the heparin lock. I looked at him and said, "I told you I wasn't kidding."

He sometimes thought I was kidding when I would stumble as I walked. He would say to me, "Walk much?" Then, I would reply with a big smile on my face, "Only for about 4 years."

NEW LIFE:
TAKE 3

T ime for a new journey, this journey was just like what every other undergraduate dreams of; I graduated from college on schedule. I graduated in May of 1994 with a BS in chemical biology, a minor in Social Science, and a mini-Masters degree in Chemical Physiology.

The only problem I had then was landing a job. I didn't want to just land a job. I wanted to find a challenging job. Not just a challenge to me intellectually, but also one that challenged me physically. I decided even though I got my degree through studying in a laboratory, I didn't want to be a person stuck in a laboratory, a "lab rat" if you will. I wanted to be someone who met interesting people and saw interesting things. I kept this in mind when I saw this job posting:

Technical Representative I for the Highly Protected Risks (HPR) Department of Insurance Company located in New York City, requirements: Bachelor's degree in either engineering or science, ability to take notes and write reports, willing to learn new skills

Position comes with salary, benefits, expense account and use of a company car

I jumped at the opportunity and submitted my resume.

I found out through the interview process the purpose behind this job was to make sure the property loses that may take place at the properties this company carried policies for was minimized, which meant I needed to learn all about property safety equipment and construction of commercial buildings. The new skill I needed to learn was a new science for me, the science of fire protection engineering which included the calculation of fire sprinkler protection grids.

It required me to climb tall buildings in a single bound (I took the elevator and walked down the stairs) inspecting everything from the roof of the building down to the basement boiler room and everything in between to be sure the subject property was protected from major loses because the value of these properties/risks was always more than $1 million.

I wasn't allowed to do this on my own, not until I was fully trained and learned this new science of fire protection engineering. The training took place in Pittsburgh, PA.

I temporarily moved to Pittsburgh. I was all by myself. I didn't know a soul there. My trainer was the only person from my company living there. He was a guy, over 40, single, and living alone. I did not feel comfortable talking to him about anything that wasn't work related. Through my job I got to see a lot of things, but mainly I had to concentrate on making sure the properties were protected from fire. I had to look for fire prevention apparatus including fire extinguishers and fire sprinklers in offices, in hospitals, even in manufacturing plants. After my inspection I was to go home and write a report of my findings and make recommendations to better protect the facilities from loses. Sometimes the recommendations were house keeping related, sometimes the recommendations were to replace the roofing materials, and sometimes the facilities got a "clean" report because the management took safety regulations seriously. When the facilities received a good report their premiums were kept low.

I was given an assignment to inspect a manufacturing plant. This plant made the coolest stuff! They made the rides for the amusement parks, including the horses for the carousel rides which were first spray painted and then the details hand-painted to make each carousel horse unique. I was excited about doing this inspection on my own, only having to report my findings to my trainer. Because it was a manufacturing plant, I had to have on all my required safety gear which included heavy steel-toed shoes, washable pants, a semi-tight fitted shirt that wouldn't get caught in machinery, a hard hat and safety glasses as well as wearing my long hair in a pony tail. I needed to bring some of my tools with me for this inspection which included a clip board with regular paper for notes, a tape measure, a flash light, a camera for taking pictures and graph paper to sketch any and all sprinkler lines for calculation while writing the report after the inspection. I carried all these supplies (plus my personal identification to prove who I was when I arrived on site and the keys to my company car) with me throughout the inspection of the 4 buildings, 1 large main building, a simply constructed rectangular steel frame building and 3 smaller out lying buildings.

I followed the plant's Safety Manager through the main building, recording everything I saw on my clipboard. I was amazed at all the safety regulations they had in place and how well everything was fitted with fire safety apparatus. I measured the size of the building using my tape measure to be sure the fire sprinkler protection I sketched on the graph paper was correct for the use and square footage of the building. The building was well illuminated for use as the office space of the business and the detailing operation that was taking place in the far corner of the building. It was so well illuminated I didn't need to use my flashlight in this building. I took pictures to prove to my trainer I was there and to update the file.

The Safety Manager then took me to the out lying buildings. These buildings weren't as clean or as well illuminated as the main building. It was in the out lying buildings that the spray painting of the carousel horses took place and the drying of said horses before they could be brought back to the main building to be detailed. I was ready to inspect these buildings with my flashlight in one hand, my clipboard with pen in the other, my bag carrying the remaining supplies over my shoulder, my hard hat on my head, my heavy steel-toed shoes on my feet and my safety glasses on my face.

I looked up trying to see if there was sprinkler protection in this building. It was hard to see, because it wasn't well lit not like the main building. I put down my bag with all my supplies in it after I put down my clipboard and flashlight then I took off my safety glasses thinking I had something on them from all the paint in the air.

I looked in the direction of the Safety Manager and said,

"I can't see."

There was a pause because I kept fiddling with my safety glasses and rubbing my eyes, then I said with a smile, "I can't see the sprinkler heads, but I'll take your word for it."

I left that inspection confused and scared. I really couldn't see. (At least not like I could the hour before) I was all alone; I didn't have any friends or relatives that lived close by. My mom was over 8 hours away.

I can handle this.

I will go to an eye doctor.

I have insurance.

I went to one of those walk-in places that accepted my insurance. I told the Eye doctor what I had experienced the day before. He gave me the eye chart test, first on my right eye.

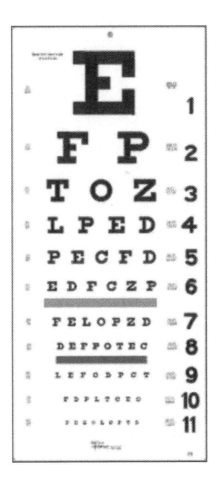

I could see perfectly with my right eye, but then he asked me to switch eyes with the plastic eye cover so he could test the left eye. I had closed both eyes to "clear" my vision for when I switched eyes.

I opened my left eye as the doctor said, "Read the smallest line you can see."

I couldn't see any lines.

I couldn't see the doctor.

I couldn't see anything.

The only thing my left eye was seeing was a clean slate of WHITE.

Is this what it feels like to be blind? Is all you can see white? What am I going to do? I can't tell my boss, they will fire me. They will think I can't do my job.

The Eye doctor didn't look as concerned as I felt. He said to me it is a good thing that you see white. He said, "If you had lost all sense of sight, you would see black." He told me to go home and rest and to return tomorrow.

When I got home to my 4th floor apartment with my eyes dilated from all the tests the eye doctor ran on me, I called home to mom in NJ. As I sat for a few more hours contemplating what was going on with my eyes, I called home again because I wanted to talk to my mom again. My dad answered the phone. He asked me how I was feeling. I answered him and then asked to speak to my mom.

He then said to me, "You can talk to her when she gets there."

"What do you mean when she gets here?" I said.

"I dropped her off at the airport about an hour ago." He said

Buzzzzttttt.

That was the sound of the intercom from downstairs to buzz people in, it was my mom. She was fast! I was still on the phone with my dad.

My mom took me back to the eye doctor the next day. It was a good thing she came because the eye doctor had called a local neurologist. This neurologist was doing his rounds at the hospital and asked us to meet him there. I would have had a heck of a time with my eyes dilated navigating myself through those unfamiliar roads to get to the hospital - never mind the hallways of the hospital had my mom not been there to drive me and then to guide me. I needed my mom there to show me the direction to walk because I could not see with one eye and the other eye was overcome with the light both from the sun and the lighting inside, sunglasses only helped a tiny bit.

This neurologist checked my eyes for himself. He said he had spoken to the eye doctor about what I was experiencing and he said because I could at least see white I was experiencing Optic Neuritis of the left eye. That was almost five years after my first supposed "MS experience." This time I couldn't argue I was too young. After all I was 22 by this time which is still young but getting closer to the age of acceptance and the normal age of MS onset.

All the other doctors I had seen in the past five years always put doubt in my mind about whether or not I had MS, feeding my denial. This neurologist asked if I had experienced anything like this before. Mom and I told him of the paralysis, of the deafness and then of the problems with my arms.

The doctor then said trying to be funny, "Now you can check off blindness from your list."

I didn't want to check off blindness!

I didn't want to check off anything!

I just wanted to cross off MS from my life!

I had to undergo yet another round of IV Solumedrol (steroids) in hope of regaining my ability to see. This time it was only for three days and then a quick taper. I agreed right away because I needed my sight to keep my job. I was able to continue to deny that MS was a part of my life because what I could keep "in the closet" was going to stay "in the closet". Immediately after the first day of the steroid treatment I could still see with my right eye although it was getting a little fuzzy (one of the side effects of steroids) but then I could also see with my left eye more than just white.

I convinced my supervisor (who was also the person that hired me) in NYC that life in Pittsburgh by myself was just not conducive to my mental state and I wished to return to NYC to continue my training. After a few strings were pulled I was able to return to NYC to work without having to divulge my secret. I didn't have to tell anyone at my job I was in the hospital or that I was "sick" at all. I didn't have to tell anyone I went blind on the job. It was none of their business. I did my job and I did it well.

That was all that mattered on the job. After taking some "personal" time to move back to the NYC area, I returned to work at the office on the 31st floor of the World Trade Center with no signs of blindness.

By the way I turned in my report that I wrote while receiving my treatment in the hospital with photos, sketches, calculations and a few recommendations for improvement at that site. The plant's Safety Manager was disappointed I wasn't the returning representative for the insurance company the following year because he wanted to show *ME* he listened to my recommendations. (I know this because it was my trainer that called and told me so.)

TIME FOR HONESTY

Things started getting serious in my life well at least in the personal department. That guy that came to see me in the hospital when we were in college… after months of joking about it, asked me to marry him. We agreed on a date to have the ceremony but now we had to go to Pre-Cana. (Pre-Cana is a Catholic course on marriage. Engaged couples need to take part in the course before they can be married in the Catholic Church.) Instead of going through weeks of meetings we decided to go on a Pre-Cana weekend together with other couples who were also getting married in the Catholic Church.

As part of the getting to know each other better before committing the rest of our lives to one another, we were each given a notebook. These notebooks were used to write the answers to the questions we were each given. We were to read the question from the piece of paper we were given; then write our answer in our own notebook in separate rooms. After writing our answers we were to join each other and switch notebooks so we would be sharing our answers. Questions we were given included, when was the first time you noticed your partner? When did you realize you wanted to marry your partner? How many children do you want to have and why? If there was something about your partner you could change; what would it be and why?

That last question is one that has come up a few times over the course of our marriage, but Chris' answer in his notebook was the most loving and caring answer. Chris wrote he would change the fact that I had MS because he loved me. When I read that answer, tears came to my eyes. He could have written anything. He could have written he wanted me to lose weight because he was tired of hearing me complain about being heavy. Instead he wished to change the fact that what the doctors had been telling me for the past ten years up to that point was not a reality. He wished to take away all the pain and the mysteries.

After pulling myself together and finally being able to hold back these tears of joy, I thanked him and said I appreciated his sentiment. I said I also knew he couldn't take it away no matter how hard he tried and I wasn't sure I would want him to take it away if he actually could. I didn't want him to take it away because having MS although I kept it to myself still guided my decisions and made me appreciate life just a little bit more than the next person. If he was able to take it away to make it not a part of my life ever, I'm not sure who this person he was planning to marry would actually be. If he could take all these ten years of journeys and experiences away from my memory banks, I don't know what journeys would be left in their place. I don't know what kind of person would be there to walk down the aisle for him to spend the rest of his life with.

After many happy tears were shed, hugs and kisses shared over that weekend, we came to the conclusion we were ready to spend the rest of our lives together.

HERE COMES MY ANGEL

The next four years were uneventful…

I switched careers… twice,…

got a dog,…

bought a house,…

got a second dog,…

got engaged,…

got married…

switched careers again…

Okay, so I was just kidding *smile* I didn't want to bore you with all the wishy-washy stuff.

Then as if some outside force said it is time for a MAJOR change in your life…

I started getting dizzy spells. Someone suggested it could be Vertigo. I wasn't sure what vertigo meant, kind of like when I was 12 and I got hit in the stomach with a soccer ball and the referee asked me if I felt nauseous.

What I did know was I hadn't seen a Neurologist in years almost 5 years, and it was probably as good a time as any.

I chose to go to the doctor that was within walking distance of my house, after all I could walk, I could see, I could hear and the weather was warm! Since this was my first visit with this new neurologist I brought with me some of the special x-ray films of my brain that showed "signs" of Multiple Sclerosis. These first films were taken by a Nuclear Magnetic Resonance (NMR) machine. Due to "fear of Nuclear anything" the name has since changed to Magnetic Resonance Imaging (MRI). On my first visit, previous M.R.I.'s in hand, I told the doctor of my previous diagnosis of MS and all the doubt still looming. Due to the years that had gone by since my last film he said he needed to see a more recent MRI Scan to also confirm for himself that I had or didn't have MS. So off I went to lie down for two to three hours in a tube in a wall or so I thought. It had been so long since my last film, I didn't realize how much more advanced MRI machines had become. This MRI was located in a trailer that was pulled up to the building and only took 1-1/2 hours to complete. Best of all my dizziness was gone!

I went back to the Neurologist to find out what the films said. I told him I was better. He saw the old lesion scars on the films. Those scars confirmed for him I had MS. He then suggested I take one of the ABC drugs (Avonex, Betaseron, Copaxone). The ABC drugs were the three options that were now available for people with MS. All three had their own advantages, but they also had one thing in common. They were all given through injection. I told him I don't like needles. Just like the same response I gave the doctor back in 1993 when Betaseron(the B of ABC drugs) was first brought to the market and I was only twenty-one years old. This time though I insisted I had only been married for one year and I had stopped taking birth control. The doctor asked me if we were trying to get pregnant.

I said, "Not on purpose but if it happens I'm not going to stop it."

So he said he wouldn't push the ABC's if my husband and I were trying because it was not suggested to be on these drugs if you were pregnant or trying to become pregnant.

He said, "Now would be a good time to try and get pregnant since you are so healthy, and during your pregnancy you will feel even stronger."

Famous last words...

My husband and I thought it would be difficult to get pregnant, because our friends had been "trying" for years and none of them had been on steroids.

One month after that visit with the neurologist, I got another test result. It was a positive result on a pregnancy test. We had a scare in the early months of the pregnancy, so I had to take it easy and rest more often then I had been. I took it easy, but I learned what being nauseous really meant. I felt nauseous for that first trimester, and felt worse during my second…then I stopped feeling anything at all from my waist down and could move even less.

At six months of pregnancy, my husband and cousin, Judy, had to carry me into my neurologist's office. He looked at me in the desk chair I was pushed in on, because there were no wheelchairs to be found, and said, "You are not supposed to be like this now, this is supposed to happen after you give birth."

He then told my husband to bring me straight to the hospital and he would call my OB/GYN to meet us there. I spent the next week in the hospital on steroids with a baby heart monitor strapped to my belly.

I thought I was going home. I just wanted to be in my own bed with my husband. They told me I would be going home as soon as I showed signs of my ability to move and feel. I was walking to the bathroom with the use of a walker, but still on my own. I could feel the cold floor under my feet and through my socks that has to be proof enough.

Then one night while having a conversation with the night nurse, my heart rate went up to 200 beats per minute which was 50 beats faster than the baby's. A normal female adult's heart rate is around 60 to 80 beats a minute. The cardiologists and the pulmonologists that were called in by the nurses tried everything physically to get my heart rate back to normal. Nothing worked so then they had to use one of the ports that was already in my veins and gave me a drug to slow down my heart rate. It worked, but I spent the next week in the Maternity Intensive Care Unit (MICU) anyway for observation.

As a patient in the MICU my husband and I had to make some decisions together because every test I underwent so did the baby. The tests that were conducted were to determine why my heart rate went up so high. Yet again, no answers.

I left the hospital in a wheelchair to protect the baby with orders to start taking insulin by injection and checking my blood sugar levels 4 times a day and eating only 1300 calories a day. I was the skinniest pregnant woman I ever knew. I actually lost ten pounds that month! The doctors weren't worried because my baby was the most photographed fetus, having a sonogram at least once a week until the day she was born, which happened a month earlier than predicted.

I actually got a refund from my Lamaze class. I called the teacher from my hospital room with baby there next to me and asked if I would still be getting my certificate.

By the way, I <u>walked</u> into the labor and delivery room, I refused a wheelchair when the orderly came out with one. I had the best Epidural. Don't worry I did my research on Epidurals. I had called an anesthesiologist before I had this bout with MS.

> I asked the anesthesiologist all the usual questions a first time mother asks but then I asked this one, "If I don't have the Epidural, and I feel all the pain associated with childbirth, will this child be a better behaved teenager?"

Needless to say, I still have no idea what a contraction feels like, because I just kept having these excruciating pains radiating down my spine. So yes, I had an Epidural.   This Epidural was so good! It was so good that the nurse had to tell me when I was having a contraction through the monitor I was hooked up to.

My husband and I had decided even though I was having the weekly sonograms that we wanted to be surprised about the gender of the baby. We had picked out a girl's name, but we hadn't decided on a boy's name. So when I told my husband, Chris, at 8 months of pregnancy my water broke, he could only respond by saying we hadn't picked out a boy's name yet.

The baby took its time to come out. My water broke at 9:45pm on Thursday night, but the baby wasn't born until 5:20pm on

Friday. When the baby did come out, it was the longest pause when the nurse said, "It's a.........................girl!" Then she turned to me and asked me what her name was.

To which I replied, "I don't know. We just met."

Here came my angel. Her name is Rachel Ashley, which was not the name we originally picked. She weighed 6 lbs. 13.5 ozs., and was 19&3/4 inches long. She was healthy, normal and not considered a preemie! Everyone was great! I didn't break daddy's hand from squeezing it every time that pain radiated down my spine. I could walk to the nurses' station. I could hold my angel without assistance. I could breast feed without difficulty. We were both released from the hospital by Sunday morning with no restrictions.

One month after Rachel was born, I went deaf again then a week later lost the use of my legs, underwent steroid treatment for a week at the hospital away from my one month old daughter. I started walking again with the use of a walker.

Then in her second month of life, I fell to the floor once more. Back to the hospital I went for another steroid treatment. While I was in the hospital this time, my neurologist suggested that if my paralyzed legs started developing spasms to ask for some Baclofin, a muscle relaxer. That first night I lay there in my hospital bed miserable trying to hold back the tears because I didn't want to be in the hospital, I wanted to be home enjoying my new baby. I wanted to be home like every other new mother waking up in the middle of the night for feedings. I even *wanted* to change dirty diapers. I *wanted* to rock the cranky baby back to sleep. I *didn't want* to be there in the hospital hooked up to a catheter, unable to get to my purse on the other side of the room. I started to cry and that is when my legs started spasming, jumping all over the place. My legs jumped so much they actually threw my blankets off of me and the bed. I called for the nurse to come in and to bring the muscle relaxer the doctor left orders for. She came in with the medicine and she fixed my blankets. She also had to adjust the catheter bag because the weight of the blanket had pulled it loose. No sooner had the nurse walked out of the room that I started experiencing my first side effect from the muscle relaxer. I started to have an asthma attack.

I wasn't worried about the asthma attack; I've had them before. It usually happens when I'm exposed to citrus. That is why I keep an emergency inhaler in my purse. The bigger problem was that my purse was on the other side of the room and I couldn't get out of the bed.

I used the call button again to get the attention of the nurse. The nurse got to the doorway of my room and panicked herself. She started calling for assistance from the other nurses on duty.

She called out some code before she would even stop to listen to what I was trying to ask for. The other nurse came running in with an oxygen mask which she immediately put on my face and then hooked it up to the oxygen port in the wall. My breathing was restored to normal within minutes. That is when I was finally able to ask for my purse from the other side of the room which I then pulled out my inhaler to show the nurse.

The next morning the doctor on duty came by to see how I was doing. He looked at my chart and saw the notes about the asthma incident from the night before.

He looked at me and said, "I don't think you should take Baclofin anymore." *No kidding!*

I walked out of that hospital again with no signs of paralysis. I returned home to my baby. I could no longer breast feed my daughter because of all the steroids I had taken. She had gotten used to baby formula and my husband had gotten used to getting up in the middle of the night to feed her.

By September of 2000, my daughter was 3 months old. Out of those first 12 weeks of her life I spent 3 of them away from her. I told my husband we needed to do something. That is when I got an appointment to start seeing the MS Specialists at the University of Medicine and Dentistry of New Jersey (UMDNJ) in Newark,

NJ. They suggested I start taking one of the ABC drugs, and since I already had been taking insulin shots during pregnancy I wasn't afraid of shots anymore. What I was afraid of was spending more time away from my daughter because I didn't do all that I could to be with her.

The doctors explained it to me in this way... MS is like an iceberg, the portion you see on the surface is tiny in comparison to the size of the iceberg that is under the water. I decided to start taking C, Copaxone, of the ABC drugs available to people with MS. My mom, my husband, as well as I got trained on how to give me this medication through injection, shots. I was to take these shots once a day until further notice. The main purpose of this medication was to treat the underlying symptoms that were taking place within my Central Nervous System (CNS), the larger portion of the "iceberg".

Everything seemed to be going well. I was walking, unassisted. I could hear from both ears. I was seeing out of both eyes and I was able to care for my daughter on my own. Then by November, I started going numb all over again as well as my vision being disrupted. The doctors at UMDNJ were going to try a different treatment to try and "trick" the MS. I agreed to try this "new" treatment. It was called Plasmaforesis. Plasmaforesis is done under the guidance of another specialist, an Oncologist. It is done through a port that is surgically placed in ones neck. This plasmaforesis procedure is actually the removal of the blood from your body and "washed" (the plasma portion of your blood is removed and replaced) and then put back in within a few hours and is usually done as an outpatient procedure.

Did I just say usually?? Did I mention that I also have allergies? And did I mention that I have odd allergies? I'm allergic to citrus. You know oranges and lemons, to name a few.

For the love of my daughter, my angel, I had the port surgically placed in my neck and went back the next week to start my treatment as an outpatient. I went through this surgical procedure so I could try to give my daughter a "normal" mom. I had to wait a week for the surgery cuts to heal before I could receive my first treatment.

I went back to the hospital one week later. No one had looked at my chart to see that I was allergic to citrus and that it causes me to have asthma. The nurse overseeing the treatment refused to give me the treatment after she asked me if I had any allergies. She refused to give me the treatment because the liquid used to replace the plasma in the blood was citrus based. They sent me home from the hospital without a treatment.

I returned the next day after receiving the phone call that they now had the correct liquid to treat me. I had undergone the treatment every day for a week with Thanksgiving in between. I needed to tell you about Thanksgiving being in between because by Thanksgiving, I had no feeling from my upper torso down and my walking was limited. I was handed a HOT cup of tea. My shaking hand spilt some of it on my belly, which resulted in a second degree burn I didn't feel.

Thinking back on this, I am glad I couldn't feel it.

I returned to the hospital for my treatments but instead of getting better, I was getting worse. So then they added steroids to the treatment.

In December of that year, my husband agreed to let me and my daughter move in with my mom to make it easier for him and her since she lived over an hour away. I have pictures of my daughter's first Christmas with me on the floor with her at my mom's house. In most Christmas photos, Mommy being on the floor with her child is not unusual but I know why I was on the floor, it was because I couldn't stand. I was lucky I could even sit up.

January 2001, the doctors at UMDNJ told me to stop taking Copaxone, the shots, because it wasn't helping and to start me on IV Ig, Intravenous Immunoglobulin. Rachel and I were still living with my mom and dad in Toms River, NJ. The latest prescription of IV Ig was to be given under the supervision of an RN. Lucky for me, I discovered that I didn't need to go to the hospital for this treatment the nurse could treat me while I sat on my mom's couch with Rachel in the play pen there next to me. By the end of my first treatment, my body started a new exacerbation/relapse. The next time the nurse came to give me my next IV Ig treatment she was also instructed to give me more solumedrol, steriods. It worked. The steroids gave me the ability to walk again, but not for long.

March 7, 2001, this was the day my husband and I closed on our new home in my mom's neighborhood and the last day I walked without assistance. I moved into my new two story home, with a hospital bed set up in the first floor living room with nurses and aides visiting me twice a day because now I was paralyzed from the neck down. Not only was I paralyzed, my vision wasn't clear, and my hearing wasn't the best.

The lowest day of my life was when at the age of 28, my 28 year old husband changed my daughter's diaper and then changed mine.

I wanted to die that day!

I wanted to close my eyes and not wake up.

I wanted it all to end.

Instead, I heard my daughter's laugh and found my will to live again. I made the decision that night that my daughter was not going to grow up without me and I was going to do everything and anything to get out of that bed!

PHASE III

THE JOURNEYS
OF ACCEPTANCE

I WILL NOT GIVE UP

In April, I underwent two weeks of Chemotherapy in yet another attempt to halt the MS in its tracks. My mom wheeled me into the local hospital for the outpatient procedure. I made friends with the nurses. I made jokes. I told them about my angel. I fell asleep for the procedure because I was lying on a bed. It didn't work. I made calls to my neurologists at UMDNJ when I got back to my mom's house and told the doctors that instead of getting better I was getting worse. I told the doctors I was losing the feelings in my body all the way up to my neck and my face was feeling as if it was losing feeling too. So again they added old reliable, steroids to the regimen. I wanted to do anything I could to get out of that hospital bed in the living room and to return to my bed that was on the second floor of our new house with my husband.

I started moving my hands, then my arms, and by Rachel's first birthday in June of 2001, I was able to sit up in my wheel chair again and sing happy birthday with just a touch of belz palsy on the right side of my face. (Belz Palsy is when the muscles in ones face are not supporting your features and it appears the face is "melting.")

On July 13, 2001, it was a day of triumph for my family. Rachel was 13 months old. She walked around the house holding onto the walls or her doll's carriage just like mommy did with her walker. But on this day, it was the day both mother and daughter took their first steps unassisted.

I started Betaseron, (B of the ABC drugs) the MS injectible medication. I was also told to take Paxil, an anti-depressant to overcome the depression that was a side effect from the Betaseron, as well as an extremely slow taper off oral steroids in August of 2001. I was able to end my use of the steroids because I could walk, I could hear, I could see, and my face was no longer hanging off the bones. As a matter of fact, my face was swollen from all the steroid use. I had chipmunk cheeks and my neck was swollen as well. In my mind it was due to the steroids. After my daughter was born in June of 2000, I weighed 180 pounds. Even though my husband, my mother, and my cousin who had been helping me all through these months all told me I had gained weight. I didn't believe them. I looked in the mirror and I still saw the same face looking back at me. I didn't see anything any different so I didn't believe them. I thought they were all just kidding around with me. I had been wearing the same clothes since Rachel was born. Granted they were sweat pants, sweat shirts and oversized T-shirts.

Yeah, my breasts were bigger but I was still swollen from lactating so much, at least that was what I kept telling myself. I wasn't wearing the normal bras, I was wearing sport bras because hooking the normal bras was still a little difficult for me to accomplish due to the lack of dexterity in my hands.

Life was good! I could care for my daughter. I could walk up the stairs to my bedroom and sleep with my husband. I could see. I could hear. I could feel. So when we got an invitation to a friend's wedding on a cruise around the Island of Manhattan, my husband and I decided I was able enough to attend.

It was September 2, 2001, that I attended that wedding with my husband. I had to purchase an outfit to wear to this wedding. The outfit was a size 22. My own wedding dress I wore only 3 years earlier was a size 14, yet I still didn't believe my husband when he said I had gained weight. It didn't make me mad when he said I was fat because those anti-depressants worked so well. They worked so well I didn't get mad, I didn't get sad, and I didn't smile. I was just there.

That Christmas we received all the usual cards and exchanged all the usual presents. We also got a thank you card from the friends whose wedding we attended in September. Along with the card was a picture of the bride and groom and a second picture of me and my husband at the wedding. Seeing that picture overcame any effects from the anti-depressants I was taking. I held up that picture and said to my husband, "Why didn't you tell me I was this fat!?!"

In January 2002, I finally ended my taper of the steroids. I made another major life decision, I took charge and told the doctors I didn't want to take the anti-depressants anymore; I told them I wanted to feel emotion. I told them I wanted to smile again.

I decided I didn't like the way I looked in that picture of me at that wedding. I took charge of my body only 6 months earlier, I wasn't lying in that hospital bed anymore. I now believed in mind over matter. If I minded then it mattered! I followed the path of a new journey, I chose to change. I changed the way I eat. I weighed 225 pounds and that bothered me, I minded so it mattered to me. I read some books on how to lose weight, but I didn't just want to lose weight I wanted to change the way my picture looked. I took more pictures of me in a bathing suit this time– I HATED THESE IMAGES. Having these images right there in front of me reminded me of what I wanted to change. I ate off smaller plates. I never ate my daughter's leftovers. I changed the order of the foods I ate. I ate proteins first then vegetables and then carbohydrates last. No portion was larger than my fist. I stopped eating when my stomach was full. I used the weight of my body to do exercises. I went through the movements that were in the books I had been reading. Overcoming an inability shows you if you want something bad enough all you have to do is take the first "step" to change it. I am not disabled, I am Differently Abled! I lost 75 pounds that year and have kept it off ever since.

I wasn't going to hide anymore! I finally accepted MS is a part of my life but it wasn't going to be my only life. I made a choice. I decided to get involved locally especially after 9/11/2001. I used to work in NYC and my office was on the 31st floor of the North Tower. Although my friends were no longer working for the company, a few of them perished because they were attending a meeting there that day. So I tried to make a difference anyway I could. I became the President of our homeowners association. I got involved in local politics; I interviewed to run for mayor, but accepted the nomination and was elected as county representative instead. I made phone calls to local radio stations. I wrote letters that were published in the community newsletters. I tried to make a difference in anyway I could.

I have had several more exacerbations/relapses ranging from paralysis of the legs, to stiffness of my writing hand, to blindness in the form of double vision. Everyday is a new adventure.

If there is anything I have learned over these last 18 years, it is that I have MS but MS does not have me. It may slow me down from time to time, but it won't stop me. I have and will continue to find the positives in life.

I admit sometimes it is hard, sometimes it is very hard!

People are surprised when I tell them I have MS. I know they are surprised because they say these words, "You look so good, you can't be sick."

Hearing those words brings a smile to my face and warmth to my heart. Those words do that because I know where I've been and I know what I have accomplished.

I know that I have had to learn to walk again several times in my life.

I know I have had to learn to be ambidextrous.

I know I can't jump rope anymore.

I know I can't run anymore.

I know I can't walk for a very long time anymore.

I know I can't drive myself very far anymore.

I know there are things I used to do and took for granted.

I have grieved my loses, but instead of feeling sorry for myself I have found other things I **_can_** do. I will continue to celebrate the little things.

I am happy I can walk from my bed to the bathroom without assistance every morning, for that I smile.

I am happy I can care for myself and my family, for that I smile.

I know I can talk about these experiences without fear, for that I smile.

I have given MS a new thing to stand for. MS stands for My Smile!

It is my smile that gets me through the rough times.

I have to admit, sometimes MS grounds me and I have to slow down.

I have to rest.

It is then that I smile for I was given another day to share in my daughter's life.

HERE WE GO AGAIN

I was doing great! My husband and I went on our first vacation since before my daughter was born. Unfortunately after I got off the plane, I had extreme difficulty navigating or even walking next to my husband, so I had to ask for a wheelchair at the hotel. Instead of this trip being a stress reliever and a way to find "my smile" with my husband, Multiple Sclerosis decided to take the spotlight once again. This can and does put A LOT of stress on a marriage.

This time after that unfortunate relapse was over; I did make it through the summer, the fall and most of the winter. That is until March of 2005, my eyes started not focusing together. I was clearly seeing two distinct images. When I saw my Neurologist, she told me what I was experiencing had a name, as a matter of fact it had two names. It was called Internuclear Ophthelmoplegia or Medial Longitudinal Fasciculary. To which I replied, "Oh, that's a relief, at least I'm not crazy!"

I was sitting in my kitchen with my husband, Chris, he was reading the newspaper as I was reading the sales flyers, but we weren't alone. Buzzing over my shoulder was a fly. That fly kept buzzing by my ear making me annoyed. I rolled by the sales flyer in order to swat the fly that was on the counter behind me over my shoulder. SWAT! went the flyer down on the counter.

"You missed," laughed Chris.

"I hit the one I saw!" I responded.

My vision returned finally after a month of wondering which image was real. I started driving again. I made it through another season with only bronchitis to contend with.

Then just as suddenly as my very first exacerbation/relapse at age 16 on the basketball court, but just before my 33rd birthday in September of 2005, I felt weak on the left side and lost my mobility on that side as well. Another round of steroids led to my recovery.

Then in October 2005, I started feeling a great sense of fatigue and an itch in my ear. This also led to a disagreement between my eyes again. Of course, more steroids but this time I started seeing a new neurologist, one closer to home and one that I had gotten a recommendation from another person who also deals with having MS in her life.

I got my vision back, but then just after the New Year 2006, I started feeling weak on the right side. After weeks of not wanting this to be true again, I finally got in to see my new Neurologist but he was on vacation, his associate ordered me another course of steroids.

That was the third relapse and third course of steroids in four months time...

It was extremely stressful for me and for my family, the 'Roid rages didn't help. Rachel, my daughter, was about 5½ years old. My fuse was extremely short and she refused to put her toys away after I had just told her to. Instead of walking away as I should have, the steroids in my system led to my yelling at her and calling her things I didn't really mean. Then I started crying and hugging her and telling her I was sorry. Her reaction which was normal for a child was fear. She was afraid of me, her mom. She wiggled her way out of my hug and ran to her dad crying.

My husband wanted me to leave. He wanted me to go to a nursing hospice. He wanted me to get out of his life and my daughter's life. He looked me dead in the eye and said, "I hate you!"

SCREECH, SMASH, BRICK WALL (poetically speaking)

Those were the last words spoken. Neither of us left the house, neither of us spoke to the other. Both of us went on with our lives not saying a word to the other. This went on for four days. On that fourth day, I got up from bed, took a shower, got dressed, put my shoes on and **WALKED** out of the house!

Before that moment I wasn't able to even walk my daughter to the corner to get her on her school bus, but at that moment I had to get out. I had to get away. I didn't trust my ability to see clearly enough to drive a car, so I walked. I walked to the corner. Then I walked to the next corner and then the next. I couldn't see because tears were flooding my eyes and still I continued to walk. I walked to the office building that was about a mile away from my front door. I went inside I put some water on my face to rinse out my eyes. I took some paper towels and I continued to walk. I walked to the Lutheran Church, another half mile away, just to sit and think and talk to God. I was now in pain after sitting there in the church for awhile; it was then I realized what I had just done. I walked a mile and a half away from home!

> "I can't walk that much to get back home", I thought to myself. I took out my cell phone and called a friend with tears in my eyes and said, "Can you please come and get me?"

After a few more minutes my friend got there, we talked and she let me cry. I told her what had happened 4 days prior and I told her how I got to the church without a car or a wheelchair or an electric scooter not even a cane. After about another hour but before my daughter got home from school, my friend brought me home. When I got there, my mother and my husband were there in the kitchen trying to figure out where I was. They both had been trying to reach me on my cell phone but I refused to answer it.

He thought I was with my mom.

My mom thought I was with him at home.

They were both stunned when I walked through the front door with my friend. Then only moments later my daughter got off the bus and walked in the house. Grandma volunteered to take Rachel so my husband and I could talk.

Talk we did. We talked about what had happened four days before. We talked about Rachel. We cried, we yelled, we hugged. I asked him if he remembered that notebook from Pre-Cana and that question. He said he did and he still wished he could take it away. He still felt he should be able to take it away.

> "Thank you for loving me so much, I wish you *could* take it away. The doctors can't take it away. All the drugs that are available today can't take it away. I don't think even Superman could take it away. So now we have a choice to make together, we could stay here in this house in New Jersey or we could move to a new house or we could leave

the state altogether. Whatever we do, we need to
do it together to get us back on track. I want to do
this together. I am with you! Are you with me?"
I said.

By the time Rachel returned home with grandma, we decided we
didn't want to continue on the path we had been on. We wanted
to resume talking to one another. We accepted the fact that we
couldn't remove MS from our lives but we wanted to continue our
lives together.

PHASE IV

THE NEWEST
JOURNEYS

TIME TO SPEAK OUT

I received a flyer from the local chapter of the National Multiple Sclerosis Society (NMSS) for a one day event to join others with MS to "Chase Away the Blues". The itinerary for the day included an unnamed motivational speaker. I got inspired to ask a question. I called the number on the flyer and spoke to the person in charge of the event.

Lisa from the mid-Jersey chapter of the NMSS said the answer to my question was possible, but we needed to discuss it in person. We scheduled a meeting for the next day at a restaurant near my home.

That meeting was only supposed to last maybe an hour continued on for 3. We talked about the early days of my being diagnosed or rather not being diagnosed. We talked about how far the medical field has come as far as treating people with MS. We talked about all the things that were in the works at the society both locally and nationally. Lisa listened to what I had to say and I asked her the question again.

I asked, "Could I be the unnamed motivational speaker for the event?"

Lisa told me about her experiences with others and she felt I would be a good representative of the kind of speaker she wanted to have speak to help chase away the blues.

Lisa was not only excited to have met me but she couldn't wait to hear me speak in front of the group at the event. Now I needed to write what I was going to say. I sat in front of my computer for a minute and then an hour then another hour and yet another hour. The hours turned into a day and then another day and yet another day. There was so much I wanted to say. So much I wanted to tell all the others that would be in that room. But wait, I didn't just want to give them my medical history of the past 33 years. That wouldn't chase away the blues, it would just make more sadness and almost make people feel sorry for me. So, I took everything I had typed on my computer and put it to the side. Then I started over.

I was having difficulty writing with a pen but I was going to write my notes on note cards so I could follow my thoughts and try not to forget the important stuff. Those three days of typing my personal medical journal got narrowed down to 39 index cards. Each card was a different color so I didn't get "lost" in my notes but then I was worried I might drop them and then get side tracked by having to put them back in order. So I found a ring similar to the ones I used to use for my paper route to keep track of my customers.

OK, now I had my notes on cards that were numbered and I had my ring to hold the cards together. I was ready. Now all I had to do was practice speaking. I practiced speaking by myself. I practiced speaking to my 5 year old daughter when she came home from school. I practiced in my sleep. I practiced to the mirror. But, I didn't practice in front of my husband and I especially didn't practice in front of my mom. I didn't practice in front of them because they were there, they lived it with me. They came on those journeys with me and knew what had happened when it happened. They had seen first hand the pain I had gone through and they knew the pain they went through. I didn't want to remind them of those times unless they wanted to be reminded.

My mom was my chauffeur the day of the event. I bribed her by offering her a massage as my caregiver. That was another part of the day, free food and massages. My mom and I arrived early so I could get comfortable with the surroundings. We chose to sit in the back of the room closest to the exit doors nearest the bathrooms, funny how I always need to be close to the bathroom no matter where I go.

Lisa was already there setting up the room. She saw me and she brought the other speaker of the day with her to introduce us. The other speaker was an older gentleman who has MS or at least that was what a doctor told him years ago but he still didn't agree with the diagnosis. This gentleman was a former teacher of Lisa's. He was her art teacher and had since retired and was now working art galleries in Northern NJ. We had some pleasant conversations about kids and his grandkids and about the world in general.

It was time for the festivities to begin. The DJ had been playing earlier to get the crowd into the mood and now it was time for Lisa to take the microphone. She introduced her boss and went over all of the scheduled events for the day. Then she introduced the other speaker, he went first because he had to leave early. His story was about listening to yourself. It was about recognizing changes in your own body and telling your doctors about them and not expecting the doctors to know everything. While listening to him my thoughts were that of dismay and sorrow. He had just been diagnosed with a fatal disease on top of MS so he really wasn't in a "good place" mentally. Then it was my turn. I was nervous but I had my notes. I didn't go first so that made me a little less nervous. So here I go.

I thanked Lisa and the Mid-Jersey Chapter for allowing me the opportunity to speak and for giving me the chance to "chase away my blues" as well as to chase away the blues of everyone in that room for at least that day. I added to the previous speaker's sentiments about listening to your body first then to your doctor's ideas, then I went into my prepared notes on the cards.

I was getting so excited hearing all the laughter and emotions that were erupting from my words then I tried to walk in front of the podium with the microphone and got a lot of feedback from the sound system. By this time I had lost my place in my notes and got so disoriented from the sounds coming through the speakers plus I was starting to feel weak from not having eaten since early that morning.

I took my note cards threw them up in the air and said, "I don't need them really, I lived all these stories."

From that I got a laugh and continued with my stories which I cut short because I announced I was hungry and lunch looked like it was ready to be eaten. I left the podium with applause and cheers sending me off to eat some lunch.

After I left the podium and returned to my table, my mom was crying, not because of what she heard but because of all the memories my words brought back to her. We hugged and then enjoyed our lunch and signed up for our massages.

As I enjoyed my lunch several people came over to me and said they had experienced similar things that my stories were talking about. Several other people said they enjoyed hearing me speak and they hope I do it again.

I was stopped when I went to the bathroom by people thanking me for speaking like I did. They said they understood. They said they had experienced similar things and others said they hadn't experienced anything like I did but they understood.

We all for that day became one person traveling on the same feet, with the same cane, in the same wheelchair. For that day we were all there for each other. There were no strangers in that room just friends that hadn't spoken before that moment.

A NEW "BUG"

C hris and I felt our lives needed a change after hitting that "brick wall". We decided the first thing we were going to do was change our surroundings. We had originally planned on living at the house we bought around the corner from my mom for a long time. It had everything we had always wanted and it was just getting to the point of being decorated the way we like it, but we agreed we were going to make a change.

That change we agreed on was to leave NJ. We agreed to consider Maryland, and after much house hunting and deep discussions about where we were headed, we agreed on Maryland.

Chris bought a house that was the same age as we were. It was a little smaller than the house we were moving out of but that was OK. Chris after closing on the house in June had it gutted. He had the half bath on the first floor removed and replaced with a handicapped accessible full bath on the first floor. I didn't ask him to do this but he said he wanted to make it easier for when and if

I won't be able to climb the stairs anymore. So when my friend who has a hard time with stairs came to visit, she would have a bathroom that accommodated her on the first floor.

So here we were in our new home in Maryland. Rachel started school. I was tired from unpacking so I spent a lot time resting on the couch. This in my husband's eyes was no different from what I had been doing in NJ. This in my husband's eyes seemed like I wasn't holding up to my end of the deal.

I continued to sit on the couch and think what was it that I had done that made me happy in the past that I could still do. That is when it hit me. I loved sharing my stories. How can I share my stories with others? I had heard about a club that helped people to feel more comfortable speaking from the front of the room, speaking from the podium. I got on the internet and looked for any and all information on being a public speaker, a motivational speaker if you will.

I found it. I found the club I was looking for. This club was not a small club. It was an international club with chapters spread throughout the United States and abroad. The name of this club was Toastmasters. I found the nearest club that I felt I could drive to without getting too lost (*I'm good at that, especially at night*). I called the number for the club to introduce myself and find out when the meetings were.

I didn't make it to the first meeting because it was raining. I was scared to go out on my own in the dark in the rain and no one else was able to take me. I did make it to the next meeting. I was a guest at that first meeting in October and I felt welcome. I felt this was something I could do. I remembered all the energy I felt after speaking for the first time in that packed room in NJ at that "Chase away the blues" event and I wanted to feel that way again. I felt the people in that room were there to help me to make me feel more comfortable speaking at the podium. I signed up that night and got the information I needed to become a speaker with Toastmasters International. The feelings I felt from the people in the room at that first meeting were confirmed when I read the following entry on www.toastmasters.org :

"The Values of Toastmasters International

Toastmasters International's core values are integrity, dedication to excellence, service to the member, and respect for the individual. These are values worthy of a great organization, and we believe we should incorporate them as anchor points in every decision we make. Our core values provide us with a means of not only guiding but also evaluating our operations, our planning, and our vision for the future.

The Vision of Toastmasters International

Toastmasters International empowers people to achieve their full potential and realize their dreams. Through our member clubs, people throughout the world can improve their communication and leadership skills, and find the courage to change.

The Mission of Toastmasters International

Toastmasters International is the leading movement devoted to making effective oral communication a worldwide reality.

Through its member Clubs, Toastmasters International helps men and women learn the arts of speaking, listening and thinking – vital skills that promote self-actualization, enhance leadership, foster human understanding, and contribute to the betterment of mankind.

It is basic to this mission that Toastmasters International continually expand its worldwide network of Clubs, thereby offering ever-greater numbers of people the opportunity to benefit from its programs."

The club I signed up with met every two weeks. They offered me a place on the agenda to give my first speech. The objective of the first speech which is called "The Icebreaker Speech" is a simple one: to begin speaking before an audience and to discover speaking skills you already have and skills that need some attention. I was told by the other members of the club and throughout the manual I had received that the icebreaker is just to tell everyone about yourself within 4 to 6 minutes.

I think I can do that but there is so much I could tell. How do I keep it down to only 4-6 minutes? I wrote a speech in my head. I wrote another speech on my computer. I even looked for my notes from the speech I gave in February 2006. I was nervous and excited. I couldn't wait to give my Icebreaker, but what am I going to say?

I couldn't sleep. The ideas kept traveling through my head like scenes from a movie, like chapters in a book. That was it! I'll tell my story like chapters in a book. I got out of bed rushed to my computer and wrote my Icebreaker speech!

Title: AN INVITATION!!!!

MY NAME IS JENNY HART AND I WROTE A BOOK.

WOULD YOU COME TO MY BOOK SIGNING?

WELL TO TELL YOU THE TRUTH, I DO HAVE A BOOK BUT NOT ON PAPER...YET!

IT DOESN'T HAVE A TITLE… YET.

IT DOESN'T HAVE A TABLE OF CONTENTS… YET.

BUT WHAT IT DOES HAVE IS SEVERAL CHAPTERS.

WHAT I WOULD LIKE TO DO TODAY IS TO MAKE YOU A PART OF THE NEXT CHAPTER!

WILL YOU COME TO MY BOOK SIGNING?

THE FIRST CHAPTER STARTED OVER 34 YEARS AGO IN JERSEY CITY, NJ.

THE SECOND CHAPTER TALKS ABOUT THE START OF ONE LITTLE GIRL'S JOURNEYS THROUGH LIFE.

THE BOOK CONTINUES TO TALK ABOUT THE JOUNEYS THAT THIS LITTLE GIRL EXPERIENCED THROUGHOUT HER LIFE.

IT TELLS THE STORIES ABOUT HOW THIS LITTLE GIRL OVERCAME MANY OBSTACLES THAT WERE THROWN HER WAY. HOW AT THE AGE OF 16 SHE SUDDENLY BECAME PARALYSED BUT THEN DANCED ON THREE INCH HEELS AT HER JUNIOR PROM.

HOW SHE GRADUATED FROM HIGH SCHOOL

WITH HONORS AND ATTENDED AND GRADUATED FROM ONE OF THE MOST PRESTIGIOUS COLLEGES IN THE COUNTRY.

THE STORY CONTINUES TO TALK ABOUT HOW THIS INNOCENT LITTLE GIRL HAD EXPERIENCED THINGS THAT NO ONE SHOULD HAVE TO EXPERIENCE EVER.

SHE EXPERIENCED BLINDNESS, DEAFNESS, AND PARALYSIS PARTIAL AND TOTAL. AND YET SHE STILL FOUND THE STRENGTH TO CONTINUE TO LIVE LIFE TO THE FULLEST.

THE JOURNEY TAKES HER ON TO MEET THE MAN OF HER DREAMS.

TO MAKE A FAMILY WITH THIS MAN.

TO HAVE A DAUGHTER AND A COUPLE OF DOGS.

NOW IT IS TIME TO START THE NEXT CHAPTER...

I WOULD LIKE TO INVITE YOU TO BE A PART OF THAT CHAPTER.

SO WILL YOU COME TO MY BOOK SIGNING?

There it was and on October 12, 2006, I gave that speech in a room with several people I hadn't met before and they gave me a standing ovation. I gave that speech and ended it with a promise. The promise I made that night is what you have been reading through all these stories. The stories of the journeys that life, my life has been on.

I caught a bug that night. I caught the public speaking bug. I needed to speak. I needed to tell my stories. I needed to share what I have been through to show others you can have a life even after you have been given a diagnosis of a disease with no cure. You can still find your smiles, one story at a time. Those smiles can spread. They can spread like wildfire. When the word gets out about how powerful making smiles can be, people will feel better knowing someone cared enough to make a phone call and the receiver of that phone call will be overjoyed by the voice on the other end of the phone line.

THE LATEST
JOURNEY

W̶e all have choices. Some of us choose to go to college right after high school. Some of us choose to go into the military. Some of us choose to get married and start a family. Some of us choose to become movie stars or singers. Sometimes, most times, the choices we make are influenced by our health or by the people around us. I made a choice; I chose to tell these stories about my journeys.

I titled this chapter 'The Latest Journey' because the journeys don't end just because this book does. MS as of this writing has no known cure. MS as of this writing has no absolute cause or any type of vaccination. Until that happens, I will still have questions. Until that happens, my brain will still be fighting my body. Until that happens, I accept this adventure known as life and I am thankful and blessed. Maybe you don't have MS and for that I am also thankful and you are blessed. Maybe you have something else that guides you through your every day journeys. Be it another medical demon or the people around you. Whatever it is, I hope you make the right choice. Not the right choice for me, but the right choice for you.

I am no expert. I did not go to medical school. I am not a doctor, MD or PhD. The only expertise I have is my life experiences. I have chosen to learn from these experiences and to not feel sorry for myself. I have chosen to use my experiences to empower me and to give me strength. I hope this book has helped to make you feel empowered and strong.

Now it is time for me to offer you another invitation? I would like to invite you to help me write about the next journey of this adventure. Drop me a line through the publisher (MorganJames Publishers, LLC) or through e-mail at my website (www.JennyHart.info) and help me to write your story as the journeys continue.

I look forward to meeting you in my journeys.

Here's to making the right choice, be it jewelry or a rag doll

(p.s. I like both)!

Oh, and for those of you who are curious, we didn't win that basketball game in 1989, but it doesn't really matter because I'm still playing in this game of life!

About the Author

JENNYLYN HART, NAMED AT BIRTH Jennylyn Marie Soler, is a daughter, sister, wife, mother, aunt, friend, author, and motivational speaker. She lived most of her life in various places throughout New Jersey, but now resides in Maryland in their three level home because she *can* walk up and down the stairs with her husband, her daughter ("her angel") and their two dogs. She goes to speak before a wide range of audiences to Make Smiles Happen because celebrating the little things is what really counts!

If you would like to hear her message of positive outlooks on life, visit her website www.jennyhart.info to find out when she can be in your area!

Appendix A

IFIDA KNOWN, THE VOICE OF EXPERIENCE, refers to these great individuals in the forward of this book. The reference of these people is a great history lesson in itself. How many more great people can you add to this list? Are they people you know or would like to know more about?

Go to the library or look on-line to find some answers about these and others you find information about. Then e-mail me through my web site www.JennyHart.info to tell me what you learned. So, let's take a journey together through history and present day...

Syrus - a Latin writer of maxims, flourished in the 1st century BC. He was an Assyrian who was brought as a slave to Italy, but by his wit and talent he won the favor of his master, who freed and educated him.

Albert Einstein – Winner of the Nobel Prize for Physics in 1921. He said, "Insanity: doing the same thing over and over again and expecting different results."

Herb Brooks – Coach of the U.S. hockey team in the 1980 Olympics. This was the team known as the "Miracle on Ice".

Mother Teresa - 1979 Nobel Peace Prize Laureate *Leader of the Order of the Missionaries of Charity.* She was told not to associate with the severally downtrodden such as those with leprosy.

Don Haskins - forever credited for revolutionizing college basketball when, in 1966, his all-black Texas Western team (now UTEP) upset the all-white Kentucky team coached by Adolph Rupp for the NCAA championship as documented in the movie, Glory Road.

Barbara McClintock - American scientist whose discovery in the 1940s and '50s of mobile genetic elements, or "jumping genes," won her the Nobel Prize for Physiology or Medicine in 1983.

Sam Walton - with his brother Bud Walton, founded Wal-Mart, the chain of discount variety stores that in the 1990s became the world's largest retailer.

Dr. Charles R. Drew - an American medical doctor and surgeon who started the idea of a blood bank and a system for the long-term preservation of blood plasma (he found that plasma kept longer than whole blood). His ideas revolutionized the medical profession and have saved many, many lives.

Ray Kroc - the founder of the McDonald's Corporation

Martin Luther King, Jr. - a famous leader of the American civil rights movement, a political activist, and a Baptist minister. In 1964, King became the youngest man to be awarded the Nobel Peace Prize for his work as a peacemaker, promoting nonviolence and equal treatment of all men. He is most famous for his speech, "I Have a Dream..."

Bill Gates - an American entrepreneur and the co-founder, chairman, former chief software architect, and former CEO of Microsoft, the world's largest software company

Montel Williams – talk show host, renowned motivational speaker, author, actor, and philanthropist, creator of The Montel Williams MS Foundation.

Mahatma Gandhi - was a major political and spiritual leader of India and the Indian independence movement through non-violent movements. One single, small, skinny man who changed the lives of millions of people without violence; without warfare.

Bonus

WHILE PREPARING FOR ONE OF Jenny's speaking engagements she had a dream. In her dream, she was able to stay in touch with those whose lives she has touched. She wanted to help others to write down their journeys and to share them with others, just as she has shared some of hers with you in this book.

That is where the Making Smiles Club idea came from. She wants to help people keep their heads up high by keeping a smile on their face! If you can stay positive and hopeful even when the world tells you otherwise... you can accomplish your dreams! Let me help you get there...

Get *for free* $150 worth of ways to reach out and stay in contact with Jenny and other readers of Jenny's Journeys:

   * One year free membership to the Making Smiles Club:

Its purpose is to show people that they are *not* alone and that they can do what the Nay Sayers said they couldn't do!

* 12 issues of the Making Smiles Newsletter- which includes stories of inspiration written by members of the Club, one may even be you!

* Weekly e-mails written by Jenny of Inspiration and Reasons to Smile!

* Audio CD downloadable to your computer of Jenny being interviewed on the radio

Ready to Join the Club?

Come visit us at:

www.MakingSmilesClub.com

To Join Today!

Testimonials

IN READING *JENNY'S JOURNEYS*, I laughed, I cried, I thought "Wow. Glad that didn't happen to me," and at times I felt like jumping up on my feet and applauding. And when I finished the book, I closed the cover with a broad, deep smile on my face – a smile, I suspect, like the one that carried Jenny through the tragedies she experienced to reach the victory she so compellingly describes. Jenny invites you on a journey; Take it with her.

E. THOMAS BEHR, PH.D.,

Author of *The Tao of Sales* and

the forthcoming *Selling with CLASS*

"READING *JENNY'S JOURNEYS* PROVIDES INSPIRATION as well as an example of perseverance. Jenny Hart's compelling account of her life is a motivational demonstration of how determination and attitude can lead to triumph."

JEFFREY THOMPSON PARKER
Author of *Flicker to Flame;*
Living with Purpose, Meaning, and Happiness

"**IF YOU HAVE THE DESIRE,** it is possible to change nearly every aspect of your life, if you really want to. The stories of Jenny's Journeys are proof positive that desire is where it all begins."

JOHN CHILDERS
Million Dollar Speaker Trainer and Author

"**JENNY MADE ME FEEL LIKE** I was there with her on her journeys. She inspired me to reach out and touch others the way her stories touched me. So reach for Jenny's Journeys then reach for a phone and send out smiles of your own to make smiles travel!"

LOIS WILLIAMS
Retired R.N. - Canada

"**THIS BOOK BROUGHT A LOT** of emotions out of me. Jenny shows that through her journeys, she is not a victim, then or now.

Her smile shows through her words. Everyone could benefit from reading about Jenny's Journeys."

MYRNA JENSEN

Mother & grandmother Canada

EVERYBODY FACES TOUGH TIMES AT one time or another… Jenny's Journeys is a beautiful and intimate journey of the highs and lows one faces when a life-altering illness shows up at your door…and how it really is possible to turn lemons into lemonade; and to see challenges as an opportunity to grow and learn. I was very moved and inspired by her stories!

JENNIFER CARTER

Speaker, Coach

AS A FORMER CBS NEWS network editor and cameraman I have worked on countless stories and have met many fascinating people. Many of those stories were about overcoming impossible hurdles. Then, I met Jenny Hart, a resilient, courageous woman who stands above the rest. Jenny willingly tells her story of struggle to give hope, strength and smiles to all those who listen. She is one of a kind.

MARK BRODIE

Producer/Director MIB Productions

"A HIGHLY READABLE PORTRAIT OF a complex and motivated young woman."

B. VEE

SeniorsEatingRight.com

READ JENNY'S JOURNEYS BEFORE YOU take a journey of your own and gain strength and courage to take one baby step after another. Organize your progress until you reach your journeys end in safety and success.

JANE-MARIE

Queen of Organization

www.QueenOfOrganization.com